THE ULTIMATE
NEW YORK YANKEES
TRIVIA BOOK

A Collection of Amazing Trivia Quizzes and Fun Facts for Die-Hard Yankees Fans!

Ray Walker

D1016659

ISBN: 978-1-953563-02-6

Exclusive Free Book

Crazy Sports Stories

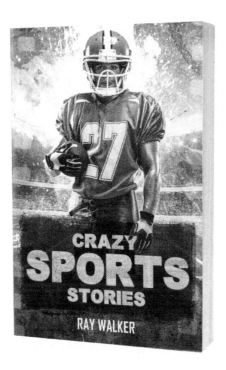

As a thank you for getting a copy of this book I would like to offer you a free copy of my book Crazy Sports Stories which comes packed with interesting stories from your favorite sports such as Football, Hockey, Baseball, Basketball and more.

Grab your free copy over at
RayWalkerMedia.com/Bonus

CONTENTS

Introduction 1

Chapter 1: Origins & History 3

    Quiz Time! 3

    Quiz Answers 8

    Did You Know? 9

Chapter 2: Jerseys & Numbers 11

    Quiz Time! 11

    Quiz Answers 16

    Did You Know? 17

Chapter 3: Famous Quotes 20

    Quiz Time! 20

    Quiz Answers 26

    Did You Know? 27

Chapter 4: Catchy Nicknames 29

    Quiz Time! 29

Quiz Answers 34

Did You Know? 35

Chapter 5: Oh Captain, My Captain 37

Quiz Time! 37

Quiz Answers 42

Did You Know? 44

Chapter 6: Statistically Speaking 46

Quiz Time! 46

Quiz Answers 51

Did You Know? 52

Chapter 7: The Trade Market 54

Quiz Time! 54

Quiz Answers 60

Did You Know? 61

Chapter 8: Draft Day 63

Quiz Time! 63

Quiz Answers 68

Did You Know? 69

Chapter 9: Odds & Ends 71

Quiz Time! 71

Quiz Answers 76

Did You Know? 77

Chapter 10: Outfielders.. 79

Quiz Time!.. 79

Quiz Answers 84

Did You Know? 85

Chapter 11: Infielders.. 87

Quiz Time!.. 87

Quiz Answers 92

Did You Know? 93

Chapter 12: Pitchers and Catchers 95

Quiz Time!.. 95

Quiz Answers 100

Did You Know? 101

Chapter 13: 27 Rings..103

Quiz Time!..103

Quiz Answers 108

Did You Know? 109

Chapter 14: The Heated Rivalries 111

Quiz Time!..111

Quiz Answers 116

Did You Know? 117

Chapter 15: The Awards Section................................**119**

Quiz Time!...119

Quiz Answers 124

Did You Know? 125

Chapter 16: The Bronx...**127**

Quiz Time!...127

Quiz Answers 132

Did You Know? 133

Chapter 17: The Babe **135**

Quiz Time!...135

Quiz Answers 140

Did You Know? 142

Chapter 18: The Iron Horse **144**

Quiz Time!...144

Quiz Answers 149

Did You Know? 150

Conclusion **152**

INTRODUCTION

The New York Yankees are one of the most storied franchises in all of sports, not only in the United States, but in the entire world. The Yankees have the most championships of any team in any sport in America. They have also had some of the best baseball players of all time play for their franchise. Even if you are not a fan of baseball or sports, chances are you know who Babe Ruth and Derek Jeter are.

The Bronx Bombers also have one of the biggest fan bases in sports. Playing in such an iconic place like the Bronx is part of this but having 27 World Series rings helps as well. Some of the most memorable moments in MLB history have to do with the Yankees or their players. As one of the oldest franchises in baseball, they have so much history and so many memories to look back on.

From Lou Gehrig, Joe DiMaggio, and Babe Ruth, to the Core Four, to today with the likes of Aaron Judge, every season has history to look back upon and marvel at. Not only are the Yankees winners, but they have constantly had players that MLB fans love to watch day in and day out.

Yes, they have a huge payroll, which allows them to acquire

some incredible baseball players. Some may think money buys you championships, but it takes heart and determination to win the World Series 27 times.

The great thing about Yankees stars are their reputation off the field as well as on. Lou Gehrig, Derek Jeter, and Mariano Rivera are perfect examples of this. They are role models you want your children to look up to and aspire to be like. They don't gloat about their success; they simply went out on the field every day and did everything they could to win... and they often did just that.

This trivia book is for the ultimate Yankees fans. Its purpose is to test your fandom knowledge, while also helping you to learn a couple new facts that will expand your knowledge of the Pinstripes.

Play Ball!

CHAPTER 1:

ORIGINS & HISTORY

QUIZ TIME!

1. Where were the Yankees originally founded?

   a. New York

   b. Los Angeles

   c. Baltimore

   d. Dallas

2. In what year did the Yankees move to New York?

   a. 1901

   b. 1903

   c. 1999

   d. 1915

3. The Yankees are the most successful franchise in North American Professional Sports History.

   a. True

   b. False

4. Which division do the Yankees play in currently?

a. American League West

b. American League East

c. National League East

d. National League Central

5. How much did Frank Farrell and Bill Devery purchase the Yankees franchise for when they moved them from Baltimore to Manhattan?

a. $5

b. $1,000,000

c. $18,000

d. $27,000

6. What name did the Yankees go by when they first moved to New York?

a. Yankees

b. Highlanders

c. Dodgers

d. Sharks

7. Where did the Yankees franchise play when they first moved to New York?

a. Hilltop Park

b. New York Stadium

c. Yankee Stadium

d. Manhattan Park

8. The Highlanders were referred to by fans as the New York Americans. Why were they later named the Yankees instead?

a. Named after a famous dog from 1913

b. Named after their former owner, John Yankee

c. Named after sports journalists who found it easier to fit in headlines

d. Named after a popular song

9. How many World Series titles did the Yankees win when they were the New York Highlanders?

a. 27

b. 2

c. 0

d. 9

10. Who purchased the Yankees in 1973?

a. George Steinbrenner

b. Derek Jeter

c. Babe Ruth

d. Bruce Springsteen

11. The New York Yankees logo is older than the team itself.

a. True

b. False

12. Who hit the first home run at Yankee Stadium?

a. Babe Ruth

b. Alex Rodriguez

c. Lou Gehrig

d. Joe Torre

13. Who threw the Yankees very first No-Hitter in 1917?

a. Mariano Rivera

b. Lou Gehrig

c. George Mogridge

d. Casey Stengel

14. In what year did the Yankees win their first World Series?

   a. 1927

   b. 1923

   c. 1955

   d. 1995

15. The Yankees moved up to Montreal, Canada briefly in 2004 when the Expos left for Washington D.C.

   a. True

   b. False

16. How much did the Yankees purchase Joe DiMaggio for from the San Francisco Seals of the Pacific Coast League?

   a. $1,000,000

   b. $100,000

   c. $50,000

   d. $10,000

17. How many numbers have the Yankees retired as of the 2019 season?

   a. 27

   b. 12

   c. 21

   d. 25

18. Yankee Stadium was demolished in 2009. What is the name of the stadium the Yankees play at currently?

a. Shea Stadium

b. New York Park

c. Big Apple Coliseum

d. Yankee Stadium

19. Who was the very first manager of the Yankees franchise?

a. Yogi Berra

b. Billy Martin

c. Joe Torre

d. John McGraw

20. How many World Series have the Yankees won as of the 2019 Season?

a. 27

b. 25

c. 10

d. 44

QUIZ ANSWERS

1. C- Baltimore

2. B-1903

3. A- True

4. B- American League East

5. C – $18,000

6. B – Highlanders

7. A- Hilltop Park

8. C- Named after sports journalists who found it easier to fit in headlines

9. C- 0

10. A – George Steinbrenner

11. A- True

12. A- Babe Ruth

13. C- George Mogridge

14. B – 1923

15. B- False

16. C- $50,000

17. C – 21

18. D – Yankee Stadium

19. D- John McGraw

20. A- 27

DID YOU KNOW?

1. The Yankees franchise was first known as the Baltimore Orioles before they made the move to New York. This has nothing to do with the Baltimore Orioles franchise of today.

2. The Yankees first ballpark in New York, Hilltop Park was made of all-wood. They also shared this ballpark at one time with their rival, the New York Giants.

3. The Yankees franchise started in Baltimore, because adding another team in New York was blocked by the New York Giants' franchise. Both franchises had to hold a peace conference in 1903 to try to settle their disputes. Their rivalry was intense.

4. Between 1921 and 1937, the Yankees and New York Giants met in the World Series five times. The Yankees won three of those matchups, while the Giants won two.

5. After the Giants left for San Francisco, and the Dodgers left Brooklyn for the City of Angels, the Yankees were the only MLB team in New York until the Mets were established in 1962.

6. The original Yankee Stadium debuted in 1923 in front of over 74,000 fans. The Yanks beat the Red Sox that day. The new Yankee Stadium, which the Yanks play in today, opened in 2009, the most recent year they won the World Series.

7. The Yankees have the most players in the Baseball Hall of Fame, with 27 total inductees. 22 of those players are memorialized in Monument Park at Yankee Stadium.

8. All of the Yankees retired numbers are memorialized in Monument Park at the new Yankee Stadium. Monument Park is an open-air museum that was replicated from one of the same name at the old Yankee Stadium.

9. Don Larsen threw the first perfect game in Yankees history. This was the only perfect game ever in the MLB postseason/World Series. It took place on October 8, 1956 against the Brooklyn Dodgers.

10. Many fans and players claimed that the old Yankee Stadium was haunted by the Yankee legends. Even Derek Jeter believed this to be true. Some wonder if they crossed the street and moved to new Yankee Stadium when the old one was demolished.

CHAPTER 2:

JERSEYS & NUMBERS

QUIZ TIME!

1. The Yankees were the first team to make numbers a permanent part of their uniforms.

    a. True
    b. False

2. The first logo for the Highlanders was "NY" in old english letters in what color?

    a. Blue
    b. Green
    c. Black
    d. Brown

3. The Yankees began wearing Pinstripes to make Babe Ruth look slimmer.

    a. True
    b. False

4. The number of pinstripes a player has on their jersey

depends on how big or small they are. How far apart are the Yankees pinstripes?

a. 1 Inch

b. 27/32 of an Inch

c. 10 Inches

d. ½ of an Inch

5. Although Number 42 was retired MLB-wide to honor Jackie Robinson, which Yankees player wore that number until he retired in 2013?

a. Alex Rodriguez

b. Mariano Rivera

c. Derek Jeter

d. Jorge Posada

6. Who is the latest Yankee to have their number retired?

a. Derek Jeter in 2017

b. Jorge Posada in 2018

c. Aaron Judge in 2019

d. Derek Jeter in 2016

7. The Yankees are the only team left in the MLB who wear their number on the sleeves of their jerseys.

a. True

b. False

8. How much were Derek Jeter's first set of pinstripes from his debut sold for in auction? (It's the most ever for a modern era jersey.)

a. $ 222,222

b. $1,000,000

c. $2, 255,900

d. $369,000

9. Which Yankees slugger had the top selling jersey in all of Major League Baseball in 2017,2018, and 2019?

a. Giancarlo Stanton

b. Aaron Judge

c. Brett Gardner

d. Aaron Hicks

10. The Yankees have retired numbers 1 through 10.

a. True

b. False

11. Nowadays we auction off used jerseys. Where were they sent back in 1915 when done being used by Yankees players?

a. Prisons for use in an inmates league

b. To family members of the players as a keepsake

c. To fans who won a contest

d. They were given to mobsters who sold them on the black market

12. In 2016, the Yankees changed their away batting helmets from a shine to gloss finish without announcing the change.

a. True

b. False

13. The Yankees are the only team in baseball that presently does not display players names on their jerseys.

a. True

b. False

14. What number did Babe Ruth wear as a Yankee?

    a. 1

    b. 3

    c. 10

    d. 17

15. Where do the Yankees Uniforms get washed?

    a. In a basement in Yankee Stadium

    b. At a 100-Year-Old Laundromat in Manhattan

    c. At a Raleigh Athletic Equipment Company Factory on Columbus Avenue in New Rochelle

    d. At a Nike Headquarters, one mile from Times Square

16. There are just 20 numbers under 100 that have never been worn by a Yankee player

    a. True

    b. False

17. The Yankees are one of only two baseball teams who do not have a third alternate jersey. They have one home uniform and one away uniform.

    a. True

    b. False

18. What are the Yankees' colors?

    a. Midnight Navy Blue and White

    b. Forest Green and Marigold

c. Wedding Gown White and Baby Blue

d. Cherry Red and Midnight Navy Blue

19. In what year did the Yankees adopt their iconic pinstripe look?

    a. 1988

    b. 1901

    c. 1915

    d. 1912

20. What number does current Yankees right fielder Aaron Judge wear?

    a. 99

    b. 11

    c. 2

    d. 75

QUIZ ANSWERS

1. A- True

2. D- Brown

3. B- False

4. B- 27/32 of an Inch

5. B- Mariano Rivera

6. A- Derek Jeter in 2017

7. B- False, Philadelphia Phillies

8. D – $369,000

9. B – Aaron Judge

10. A- True

11. A- Prisons for use in an inmates league

12. A- True

13. B- False

14. B – 3

15. C – At a Raleigh Athletic Equipment Company Factory on Columbus Avenue in New Rochelle

16. A – True

17. A – True, the other team is the Detroit Tigers

18. A- Midnight Navy Blue and White

19. C- 1915

20. A- 99

DID YOU KNOW?

1. The Yankees have a very strict dress code/appearance policy. It was started by George Steinbrenner in 1973. The policy states: "All players, coaches and male executives are forbidden to display any facial hair other than mustaches (except for religious reasons), and scalp hair may not be grown below the collar. Long sideburns and "mutton chops" are not specifically banned."

2. The Yankees have retired 21 numbers overall in Monument Park: #1 (Billy Martin), #2 (Derek Jeter), #3 (Babe Ruth), #4 (Lou Gehrig), #5 (Joe DiMaggio), #6 (Joe Torre), #7 (Mickey Mantle), #8 (Yogi Berra & Bill Dickey), #9 (Roger Marris), #10 (Phil Rizzuto), #15 (Thurmon Munson), #16 (Whitey Ford), #20 (Jorge Posada), #23 (Don Mattingly), #32 (Elston Howard), #37 (Casey Stengel), #42 (Jackie Robinson & Mariano Rivera), #44 (Reggie Jackson), #46 (Andy Pettitte), #49 (Ron Guidry) and #51 (Bernie Williams).

3. The first interlocking 'NY' logo that the Yankees used was originally created to be put on a medal for the first New York City police officer shot in the line of duty. It was not created for the Yankees at all.

4. Despite the fact that the Yankees do not include names on the backs of their jerseys, you can still buy Yankees jerseys with the players' names on the back. Some fans even get customized jerseys with their own names on the back.

Others find it appalling that this is even offered since the Yanks are known for only including numbers on their jerseys.

5. The only significant change the Yankees have made to their jerseys since 1913 is that they were changed from pullover style to button up, which all teams switched to. Their uniforms and simple and iconic and are rarely ever updated or changed.

6. The only time modern Yankee players get to wear their names on their backs are during MLBPA's Players Weekend in August. They are allowed to display their nicknames for fun, along with every other MLB team.

7. In 2019, a Babe Ruth Yanks jersey sold for $5,640,000. This is a record price for any piece of sports memorabilia... ever.

8. There is only one single digit number left that is not retired by the Yankees. That number is 0. In 2019, Adam Ottavino was the first player to wear the final available single digit on a pinstriped jersey. Many thought Derek Jeter would be the last to ever do so.

9. Mariano Rivera was the last player to ever wear No. 42 in Major League Baseball. 50 years after Jackie Robinson broke the color barrier in baseball, his No. 42 was retired across all 30 teams. Rivera was allowed to continue to wear the number until his retirement, because he was "grandfathered" into wearing it since it was already his uniform number when it was retired across the MLB.

10. The Yankees have 21 numbers retired, which makes them No. 2 on the list of most retired numbers in all of professional sports. The Boston Celtics of the NBA have 22 numbers retired. Both teams have 22 players retired though. (Mariano Rivera and Jackie Robinson both are retired under 42.)

CHAPTER 3:

FAMOUS QUOTES

QUIZ TIME!

1. Which Yankees player was quoted as saying, "I want to thank the Good Lord for making me a Yankee."?

   a. Derek Jeter

   b. Babe Ruth

   c. Joe DiMaggio

   d. Lou Gehrig

2. In his infamous 'Luckiest Man' speech, Lou Gehrig was quoted as saying, "Today I consider myself the luckiest man on the face of the _____."

   a. Planet

   b. Earth

   c. Globe

   d. World

3. Which Yankee was quoted as saying "Baseball is 90% mental. The other half is physical."?

   a. Yogi Berra

b. Johnny Damon

c. Jason Giambi

d. Joe DiMaggio

4. Yankees Owner, George Steinbrenner was one quoted as saying "Owning the Yankees is like owning the _____."

   a. Newest Lamborghini

   b. MLB

   c. Most Expensive Diamond in the World

   d. Mona Lisa

5. Which Ernest Hemingway novel contains the quote, "Have Faith in the Yankees, my son."?

   a. A Farewell to Arms

   b. For Whom the Bell Tolls

   c. The Old Man and the Sea

   d. Men Without Women

6. Which former Boston Red Sox pitcher was quoted as saying, "Most guys who don't like me are Democrats or Yankee fans."?

   a. Pedro Martinez

   b. Tim Wakefield

   c. Mike Timlin

   d. Curt Schilling

7. Catfish Hunter once said, "If you open a Reggie bar, it tells you how good it is." Reggie Bars were made in honor of Reggie Jackson. What did those candy bars consist of?

   a. Peanut Butter and Dark Chocolate

b. Milk Chocolate, Peanuts, and a Caramel Center

c. White Chocolate, Rice Cereal, and a Peanut Butter Center

d. Milk Chocolate, Caramel, and Walnuts

8. After a loss to the Yankees, Boston Red Sox Pitcher, Pedro Martinez was once quoted as saying he would "just tip the cap and call the Yankees my daddy."

   a. True

   b. False

9. Which rapper included the lyrics "I made the Yankee hat more famous than a Yankee can" in his song, 'Empire State of Mind' feat. Alicia Keys?

   a. Drake

   b. Eminem

   c. Jay- Z

   d. Chance the Rapper

10. Which Yankees Manager is quoted as saying "You're always in the storm's eye, so to speak, when you're with the Yankees."?

    a. Joe Torre

    b. Joe Girardi

    c. Billy Martin

    d. Buck Showalter

11. Third baseman, Graig Nettles once said, "When I was a little boy, I wanted to be a baseball player and join the _____. With the Yankees, I've accomplished both."

a. Army

b. Peace Corp

c. Circus

d. WWE

12. In which baseball movie is Babe Ruth's ghost quoted as saying, "Heroes get remembered, but legends never die."

   a. Fever Pitch

   b. Moneyball

   c. The Sandlot

   d. Major League

13. Which Yankees Hall of Famer said, "The great thing about being a Yankee is that you're always a Yankee."?

   a. Mariano Rivera

   b. Dave Winfield

   c. Whitey Ford

   d. Derek Jeter

14. Which Yankees pitcher said, "Never is a concept the Yankees won't ever come across."?

   a. Andy Pettitte

   b. CC Sabathia

   c. Mariano Rivera

   d. Goose Gossage

15. Which Yankees catcher said, "I could never wear another uniform. I will forever be a Yankee."?

   a. Yogi Berra

   b. Thurmon Munson

c. Jorge Posada

d. Bill Dickey

16. Derek Jeter once said, "Never allow the fear of striking out keep you from playing the game."

    a. True

    b. False

17. Which Yankee said "I've never been an actor on Broadway, but it feels like you're on a stage when you play at Yankee Stadium."?

    a. Derek Jeter

    b. Babe Ruth

    c. Alex Rodriguez

    d. Aaron Judge

18. Which outfielder said, "I feel like I've been a Yankee my whole life."?

    a. Bernie Williams

    b. Dave Winfield

    c. Johnny Damon

    d. Curtis Granderson

19. After winning the 2009 World Series, which infielder was quoted as saying, "I have three beautiful children and a World Series ring. That's all I need."?

    a. Mark Teixeira

    b. Derek Jeter

    c. Robinson Cano

    d. Alex Rodriguez

20. Joe DiMaggio once said, "A life is not important except in the impact it has on other lives."

    a. True
    b. False

QUIZ ANSWERS

1. C- Joe DiMaggio

2. B – Earth

3. A- Yogi Berra

4. D – Mona Lisa

5. C- The Old Man and the Sea

6. D- Curt Schilling

7. B- Milk Chocolate, Peanuts, and a Caramel Center

8. A- True

9. C- Jay-Z

10. A- Joe Torre

11. C- Circus

12. C- The Sandlot

13. D- Derek Jeter

14. A- Andy Pettitte

15. C – Jorge Posada

16. B – False, Babe Ruth

17. A- Derek Jeter

18. C- Johnny Damon

19. A- Mark Teixeira

20. B- False, Jackie Robinson

DID YOU KNOW?

1. Yogi Berra was famous for his "Yogi-isms". He said the funniest things that usually either didn't quite make sense or were super sarcastic. He was an amazing player and coach, but he is known for many of his quotes as well. A few examples: "Pair up in threes." "It's déjà vu all over again." "You should always go to other people's funerals, otherwise, they won't come to yours."

2. In the movie, Fever Pitch starring Jimmy Fallon and Drew Barrymore, Fallon's character has his friends do a dance off in order to receive tickets to a Red Sox game against the Yankees. His character, Ben tells his friends, "That's not Yankee dancing! That's Devil Ray dancin'!"

3. Babe Ruth once said, "Baseball was, is, and always will be to me the best game in the world." Babe Ruth has some of the most iconic baseball quotes of all time.

4. When Yankee fan and Comedian, Adam Sandler was asked how he'd like to die, he replied, "If I got to pick how I die, I'm praying it's at a Yankee game and a foul ball to the head."

5. The Yankees made it to the 2001 World Series, shortly after the 9/11 attacks on the World Trade Center. Ground Zero is only a few miles from Yankee Stadium. President George Bush threw out the first pitch in a bulletproof vest for Game 3 and was quoted as saying, "There was some

suggestion that maybe the best place to go would be Arizona since that's where Game 1 was being played. I rejected that out of hand. If you're going to throw out a pitch during a World Series with the Yankees at this point in history there's only one place to go – Yankee Stadium."

6. Hall of Fame Shortstop, Derek Jeter once said, "There may be people who have more talent than you, but there's no excuse for anyone to work harder than you do- I believe that."

7. Derek Jeter also once said (in reference to being a Yankee), "God, I hope I wear this jersey forever." His hope came true.

8. Olympic Medalist, Jim Thorpe once said, "The Yankees, you see, they're a money team, they're the class of baseball. You don't ever bet against that."

9. "He'd give you the shirt off his back. Of course, he'd call a press conference to announce it." – Catfish Hunter on Reggie Jackson

10. Red Sox star, Nomar Garciaparra once said, "You know it as soon as you walk in Yankee Stadium. The electricity is there every time, every day."

CHAPTER 4:

CATCHY NICKNAMES

QUIZ TIME!

1. Which of these nicknames did Babe Ruth go by? 1) The Decent Bambino 2) The Swinging Swat 3) The Sultan of Swat 4) The Incredible Bambino 5) The Great Bambino

    a. 1 & 2

    b. 2 & 4

    c. 3 & 5

    d. None of the Above

2. "Babe" Ruth is his birth name.

    a. True

    b. False

3. "Yogi" was a nickname. What is Yogi Berra's real name?

    a. Tom Daniel Berra

    b. Jacob James Berra

    c. Michael Edward Berra

    d. Lawrence Peter Berra

4. What nickname does former Yankees 3rd Baseman, Alex Rodriguez go by?

   a. Al-Roddy
   b. Alexander the Great
   c. A-Rod
   d. Ale-Rod

5. Which is a nickname the Yankees as a team are commonly referred to as?

   a. The Bronx Bombers
   b. The New York Nemesis
   c. The Manhattan Marauders
   d. The American Dreamers

6. Pitcher, James Augustus Hunter went by which nickname?

   a. Tuna Fish
   b. Catfish
   c. AquaMan
   d. Sword Fish

7. Lou Gehrig's two nicknames were "Biscuit Pants" and "The Iron Horse".

   a. True
   b. False

8. Reggie Jackson was referred to as Mr. October for his postseason contributions to the Yankees. What was Derek Jeter's postseason nickname?

   a. Mr. Postseason
   b. Mr. October 2

c. Mr. November

d. Mr. World Series

9. Which former Yankee went by the nickname, "Godzilla"?

   a. Hideki Matsui

   b. Mickey Mantle

   c. Rickey Henderson

   d. Nick Swisher

10. What was Yankees owner, George Steinbrenner called by players and fans?

    a. The King

    b. The Man

    c. The Big Apple

    d. The Boss

11. "Goose" is a nickname. What is former Yankees pitcher, Goose Gossage's real name?

    a. Maxwell William

    b. Richard Michael

    c. Kevin Arthur

    d. Bartholomew Robert

12. "Donnie Baseball" was a nickname Don Mattingly went by during his playing career.

    a. True

    b. False

13. What was the nickname of the style of play that Billy Martin loved to play with?

    a. Crazyball

b. Martinball

c. Billyball

d. Bloodyball

14. What was Derek Jeter's nickname?

    a. The Big Apple

    b. Jumping Jeter

    c. The Captain

    d. Daunting Derek

15. Which relief pitcher was nicknamed "Sandman" after using the Metallica song, "Enter Sandman" as his entrance song from the bullpen?

    a. Aroldis Chapman

    b. Phil Coke

    c. David Robertson

    d. Mariano Rivera

16. For Player's Weekend in 2019, Aaron Judge used his nickname "BAJ", which he was given during his time playing for Fresno State. What does BAJ stand for?

    a. Big Aaron Judge

    b. Big Apple Judge

    c. Bomb Aaron Judge

    d. Bad Ass Judge

17. Former Yankees Catcher, Jorge Posada went by the nickname, Posie during his playing days.

    a. True

    b. False

18. Who were a part of the "Core Four"?

    a. Derek Jeter, Alex Rodriguez, Mariano Rivera, Johnny Damon
    b. Derek Jeter, Mariano Rivera, Jorge Posada, Andy Pettitte
    c. Mickey Mantle, Babe Ruth, Lou Gehrig, Joe DiMaggio
    d. Dave Winfield, Bernie Williams, Reggie Jackson, Derek Jeter

19. "Lefty" was a nickname for Yankees pitcher, Vernon Louis Gomez. What other nickname did he go by?

    a. Dopey
    b. Scooby
    c. Loopy
    d. Goofy

20. Edward Charles Ford went by the nickname, "Whitey" due to his blond hair.

    a. True
    b. False

QUIZ ANSWERS

1. C- 3 & 5

2. B- False, George Herman Ruth

3. D- Lawrence Peter Berra

4. C- A-Rod

5. A – The Bronx Bombers

6. B- Catfish

7. A- True

8. C- Mr. November

9. A- Hideki Matsui

10. D- The Boss

11. B – Richard Michael

12. A – True

13. C- Billyball

14. C- The Captain

15. D- Mariano Rivera

16. A – Big Aaron Judge

17. B- False

18. B- Derek Jeter, Mariano Rivera, Jorge Posada, Andy Pettitte

19. D- Goofy

20. A – True

DID YOU KNOW?

1. Current Yankees Outfielder, Aaron Judge is nicknamed "All Rise" by fans due to his last name. He even created a charity called the All Rise Foundation after the nickname. Yankees fans even created a section of the stadium in right field called "The Judge's Chambers". The fans that sit in these 18 seats wear black robes, wigs, and don foam gavels.

2. Mariano Rivera is often referred to as simply "Mo".

3. Dave Winfield was nicknamed "Daddy Longlegs" after his long legs, size, and his domination out in right field.

4. Babe Ruth is known by over 20 nicknames, some more popular than others. Babe is one of them, but some of the less popular ones include: "The Wizard of Whack", "The King of Swing", "Herman the Great", and the "Mauling Menace".

5. Many fans of other teams call the Yankees "The Evil Empire" in reference to the Star Wars movies.

6. Derek Jeter was nicknamed "The Captain" and "Captain Clutch". He embodied everything a team caption should, so to honor him, the Yankees have yet to announce a new Captain since his retirement in 2014.

7. The Yankees of the late 1920's were considered some of the best baseball teams of all time. The nickname "Murderers'

Row" was given to these teams in reference to the first six hitters of the Yank's lineup: Earle Combs, Mark Koenig, Babe Ruth, Lou Gehrig, Bob Meusel, and Tony Lazzeri.

8. Some of the best nicknames past Yankees went by include: Noodles, Bubbles, Goose, Cuddles, Snuffy, Catfish, Slow Joe, Cozy, Truck, Home Run, Chicken, Bullet Joe, Sad Sam, Honey, Kiddo, and Jumbo.

9. Former Yankees Outfielder, Curtis Granderson goes by the hilarious nickname, "The Grandyman".

10. Some other team nicknames for the Yankees include: The Bronx Zoo, The Damn Yankees, The Pinstripers, and The Stankees. (The last one is obviously only used by fans of other teams.)

CHAPTER 5:

OH CAPTAIN, MY CAPTAIN

QUIZ TIME!

1. Where did Derek Jeter go to college?

    a. San Diego State University

    b. Florida State University

    c. University of Michigan

    d. He was drafted out of high school

2. Derek Jeter is the only MLB player in history to win both the All-Star Game MVP and the World Series MVP in the same season.

    a. True

    b. False

3. Derek Jeter has a charity foundation that helps kids stay healthy, be successful, become leaders, and stay out of trouble. What is his charity called?

    a. High Socks for Hope

    b. Turn 2 Foundation

    c. The Derek Jeter Foundation

    d. The Pitch-In Foundation

4. How many times was Derek Jeter an American League All-Star?

    a. 7
    b. 10
    c. 15
    d. 14

5. Derek Jeter has played the most games in New York Yankees history, at 2,747 games total.

    a. True
    b. False

6. How many Gold Glove Awards does Derek Jeter have?

    a. 3
    b. 10
    c. 5
    d. 7

7. Derek Jeter was unanimously voted into the Baseball Hall of Fame.

    a. True
    b. False

8. Derek Jeter is presently part-owner of which MLB team?

    a. Washington Nationals
    b. Oakland Athletics
    c. Los Angeles Dodgers
    d. Miami Marlins

9. Derek Jeter launched a website days after his retirement

that allows athletes from all sports to write first person articles. What is the name of that website?

a. Players' Illustrated
b. The Players' Tribune
c. Players' Point of View
d. The Players' Perspective

10. What year was Derek Jeter named 'Captain' of the Yankees?

a. 2001
b. 2003
c. 1999
d. 2007

11. Who was Jeter's favorite baseball player when he was growing up?

a. Dave Winfield
b. Rickey Henderson
c. Ozzie Smith
d. Tony Gwynn

12. Derek Jeter has hosted Saturday Night Live.

a. True
b. False

13. Jeter's 3,000th hit was a

a. Single
b. Double
c. Triple
d. Home Run

14. Derek Jeter has his own publishing company under Simon and Schuster called 'Jeter Publishing'

    a. True
    b. False

15. Which TV sitcom did Derek Jeter make his acting debut on (playing himself)?

    a. The King of Queens
    b. Modern Family
    c. Everybody Loves Raymond
    d. Seinfeld

16. In 2006, Jeter launched a men's cologne with popular beauty brand, Avon. What was the name of that cologne?

    a. Leader
    b. Focused
    c. Driven
    d. Determined

17. What other sport did Derek Jeter play in high school?

    a. Basketball
    b. Football
    c. Soccer
    d. Golf

18. How many World Series did Jeter win with the Yankees?

    a. 9
    b. 2
    c. 5
    d. 7

19. In what film did Derek Jeter make his movie debut (playing himself)?

    a. Men in Black

    b. Grown Ups

    c. The Other Guys

    d. The Hangover

20. Derek Jeter never played in the World Baseball Classic.

    a. True

    b. False

QUIZ ANSWERS

1. D- He was drafted out of high school

2. A – True

3. D – 8

4. D- 14

5. A- True

6. C – 5

7. B – False, He was shy one vote from being inducted unanimously

8. D – Miami Marlins

9. B- The Players' Tribune

10. B – 2003

11. A- Dave Winfield

12. A – True

13. D – Home Run

14. A- True

15. D- Seinfeld

16. C- Driven

17. A- Basketball

18. C – 5

19. C- The Other Guys

20. B – False, He played in 2006 and 2009- He was the
    Captain of the 2009 team

DID YOU KNOW?

1. About a year after his retirement, Jeter proposed to his girlfriend Hannah Davis. They wed in 2016 and had a daughter in 2017 named Bella Raine Jeter.

2. In his junior high yearbook, students were asked to write what they planned to be doing in 10 years. Jeter answered, "playing shortstop for the New York Yankees."

3. Jeter only struck out once during his senior year season in high school. He batted .508 with 23 RBIs, 21 walks, and 4 home runs.

4. Jeter finished his MLB career with a .310 lifetime batting average and 3,465 hits.

5. Jeter only ever used one type of bat his entire career, because of its close resemblance to a metal bat, which he was used to using in high school. In all of his over 14,000 plate appearances in the MLB, he used a Louisville Slugger P72.

6. Here are a few things Jeter never did in his career: hit for the cycle, win a regular season MVP Award, start a game 5th or 6th on the batting order, hit an extra innings triple.

7. When Jeter was drafted by the Yankees, he signed for $800,000. His signing included a stipulation that the Yankees would pay for Jeter's college education if he suffered a career-ending injury that forced him to leave baseball behind.

8. Jeter was born in New Jersey but grew up in Michigan. In 2016, he was inducted into the Michigan Sports Hall of Fame.

9. Back in 1999, limited edition 'Jeter's Frosted Flakes' cereal was produced with profits benefitting the Turn 2 Foundation. There were only 250,000 boxes made.

10. Jeter played high school basketball against NBA stars Jalen Rose and Chris Webber. Jeter won 5 championships during his career. Rose and Webber won none.

CHAPTER 6:

STATISTICALLY SPEAKING

QUIZ TIME!

1. Babe Ruth holds the New York Yankees franchise record for the most home runs. How many did he hit?

    a. 601
    b. 659
    c. 555
    d. 710

2. Andy Pettitte has the most wins in New York Yankees franchise history.

    a. True
    b. False

3. How many times have the Yankees made the playoffs in franchise history?

    a. 50 times
    b. 34 times
    c. 27 times
    d. 55 times

4. Which former Yankee comes in first all time in ERA in franchise history at 2.21?

   a. Russ Ford
   b. Jack Chesbro
   c. Mariano Rivera
   d. George Mogridge

5. Which pitcher has the most strikeouts in Yankees franchise history?

   a. CC Sabathia
   b. Lefty Gomez
   c. Andy Pettitte
   d. Whitey Ford

6. Which player has the most RBI's in Yankees franchise history with 1995 total?

   a. Lou Gehrig
   b. Babe Ruth
   c. Joe DiMaggio
   d. Mickey Mantle

7. Joe McCarthy is the Yankees all-time winningest manager in franchise history.

   a. True
   b. False

8. Mariano Rivera obviously has the most saves in Yankees franchise history with 652. Who has the second most saves in franchise history with 224?

   a. Dave Righetti

b. Aroldis Chapman

c. Goose Gossage

d. David Robertson

9. Who holds the single season Yankees record for stolen bases with 93?

a. Derek Jeter

b. Rickey Henderson

c. Johnny Damon

d. Giancarlo Stanton

10. Who holds the single season Yankees record for hits with 238?

a. Derek Jeter

b. Dave Winfield

c. Mickey Mantle

d. Don Mattingly

11. Who holds the single season Yankees record for home runs with 61?

a. Alex Rodriguez

b. Roger Maris

c. Babe Ruth

d. Lou Gehrig

12. Alex Rodriguez hit the most sacrifice flies in Yankees all-time franchise history.

a. True

b. False

13. Which pitcher has the most losses In Yankees franchise

history with 139?

- a. Red Ruffing
- b. Ron Guidry
- c. Mike Mussina
- d. Mel Stottlemyre

14. Which pitcher threw the most complete games in Yankees franchise history with 261?

- a. Lefty Gomez
- b. Red Ruffing
- c. Spud Chandler
- d. Jack Chesbro

15. Who is the most intentionally walked Yankee of all time?

- a. Don Mattingly
- b. Jorge Posada
- c. Robinson Cano
- d. Derek Jeter

16. Which pitcher has the highest WAR in Yankees history?

- a. Mariano Rivera
- b. Andy Pettitte
- c. Lefty Gomez
- d. Mike Mussina

17. CC Sabathia has hit the most batters in Yankees franchise history.

- a. True
- b. False

18. Which player has the most plate appearances all time in Yankees franchise history?

    a. Babe Ruth
    b. Bernie Williams
    c. Derek Jeter
    d. Yogi Berra

19. Which two pitchers are tied for the most starts in Yankees franchise history?

    a. Andy Pettitte and Red Ruffing
    b. Lefty Gomez and CC Sabathia
    c. Red Ruffing and Whitey Ford
    d. Whitey Ford and Andy Pettitte

20. Whitey Ford threw the most shutouts in Yankees history with 45 total.

    a. True
    b. False

QUIZ ANSWERS

1. B- 659

2. B- False, Whitey Ford

3. D- 55 times

4. C – Mariano Rivera

5. C- Andy Pettitte

6. A- Lou Gehrig

7. A- True

8. A- Dave Righetti

9. B – Rickey Henderson

10. D – Don Mattingly

11. B- Roger Maris

12. B- False, Don Mattingly

13. D- Mel Stottlemyre

14. B- Red Ruffing

15. A- Don Mattingly

16. A – Mariano Rivera

17. B – False, Jack Warhop

18. C – Derek Jeter

19. D- Whitey Ford and Andy Pettitte

20. A – True

DID YOU KNOW?

1. Derek Jeter holds the No. 1 spot for both hits and doubles in franchise history, but Lou Gehrig holds the spot for the most triples.

2. Babe Ruth has the best career batting average in Yanks franchise history at a whopping .349. Lou Gehrig holds the second spot at a career batting average of .340.

3. Derek Jeter played in 2,747 games in his career. There are only 162 games per season in the MLB. Jeter played for 20 seasons total.

4. Lou Gehrig has the most extra-base hits in franchise history with 1,190. Babe Ruth was only one behind him with 1,189.

5. Derek Jeter holds the record for most plate appearance in Yankees history with an incredible 12,602 total. Pete Rose has the most plate appearances in MLB history with 15,890. That many plate appearances are synonymous with a great player and a long, successful career.

6. Whitey Ford threw the most wild pitches in Yankees history with 75 total. He only balked 5 times in his career though.

7. Andy Pettitte allowed the most home runs in Yankees history in his career with 236 allowed. CC Sabathia is right behind him with 232.

8. Whitey Ford holds the Yankees record for most innings pitched at 3,170.1. Close behind him is Red Ruffing with 3,168.2.

9. Most people assume Rickey Henderson holds the No.1 spot on the list of most stolen bases in Yanks history, but it's actually Derek Jeter, once again. Jeter had 358 stolen bases in his Yanks career, whereas Rickey had 326 as a Yankee. Rickey holds this record for the Oakland A's and is No.1 on the MLB All-Time Stolen Bases list.

10. Babe Ruth scored the most runs all-time in Yankees history with 1,959 total. The Yanks have 12 players who all scored over 1,000 runs in their Yankee careers.

CHAPTER 7:

THE TRADE MARKET

QUIZ TIME!

1. The Red Sox traded Babe Ruth to the Yankees for $125,000 in 1920. From then on until 2004, the Yankees had won 26 World Series, while the Red Sox had won none. Many Red Sox fans blamed this on the _____.

   a. Curse of the Bambino
   b. Curse of the Babe
   c. Curse of the Century
   d. Curse of the Sultan of Swat

2. In 1999, the Yankees traded David Wells, Homer Bush, and Graeme Lloyd to the Toronto Blue Jays for which pitcher?

   a. Roy Halladay
   b. Roger Clemens
   c. Billy Koch
   d. Andy Pettitte

3. In 2004, the Yankees traded Alfonso Soriano to the Texas Rangers for which infielder?

a. Jason Giambi
b. Mark Teixeira
c. Alex Rodriguez
d. Michael Young

4. In a blockbuster, 3-team trade in 2009, the Detroit Tigers acquired Max Scherzer, Austin Jackson, Phil Coke, and Daniel Schlereth. The Arizona Diamondbacks acquired Ian Kennedy and Edwin Jackson. The Yankees acquired one player. Who was that outfielder?

a. Nick Swisher
b. Curtis Granderson
c. Melky Cabrera
d. Hideki Matsui

5. In 2000, the Yankees wanted to trade for Sammy Sosa from the Chicago Cubs, but they felt the Cubs were asking for too much. Instead, they traded with the Cleveland Indians for which outfielder?

a. Kenny Lofton
b. Manny Ramirez
c. Dave Roberts
d. David Justice

6. After a horrendous 2008 season, the Yankees overhauled players and traded for Nick Swisher from which team? Swisher was a huge part of the 2009 World Series Championship.

a. Oakland A's
b. Chicago White Sox

c. Detroit Tigers

d. Atlanta Braves

7. In 2017, the Yankees traded Starlin Castro, Jose Devers, and Jorge Guzman to the Miami Marlins in exchange for which star outfielder?

a. Giancarlo Stanton

b. Aaron Judge

c. Jacoby Ellsbury

d. Brett Gardner

8. Mickey Mantle and Roger Maris were nicknamed the "M&M Boys". Who did the Yanks acquire Roger Maris from in 1959?

a. St. Louis Cardinals

b. Los Angeles Dodgers

c. Milwaukee Braves

d. Kansas City Athletics

9. How many players did the Yankees send to the A's in their trade to acquire Rickey Henderson?

a. 5

b. 2

c. 1

d. 3

10. The Yankees acquired late 1990's dynasty hero, RF Paul O'Neill from the Cincinnati Reds in 1992.

a. True

b. False

11. Since the 30-team era began in 1998, how many trades have the Yankees made with the Arizona Diamondbacks?

    a. 0 trades

    b. 7 trades

    c. 15 trades

    d. 3 trades

12. The Yankees traded with the Red Sox back in 1997. They did not make another trade with each other until 2014.

    a. True

    b. False

13. In 2012, the Yankees traded Danny Farquhar and D.J. Mitchell to the Seattle Mariners for which longtime Mariner?

    a. Justin Smoak

    b. Ichiro Suzuki

    c. Felix Hernandez

    d. Kyle Seager

14. The Yankees have only made 3 trades with the Tampa Bay Rays ever.

    a. True

    b. False

15. In 2019, Nick Swisher came out of retirement and signed with the Yankees, only to be traded 10 games later back to the Cleveland Indians.

    a. True

    b. False

16. In 2014, the San Diego Padres traded _____ to the Yankees. The Yanks traded him back to the Padres in 2017.

    a. Yangervis Solarte
    b. Shawn Kelley
    c. Chase Headley
    d. Chad Gaudin

17. In 2018, the Yankees acquired Andrew McCutchen and cash considerations from which team?

    a. Colorado Rockies
    b. Pittsburgh Pirates
    c. Philadelphia Phillies
    d. San Francisco Giants

18. In 1990, the Yankees traded Dave Winfield to which West Coast team?

    a. California Angels
    b. Oakland Athletics
    c. San Diego Padres
    d. Los Angeles Dodgers

19. In 1995, the Yankees purchased Rick Honeycutt from the _____. Two months later, the _____ purchased him from the Yankees.

    a. Texas Rangers, Oakland Athletics
    b. St. Louis Cardinals, Oakland Athletics
    c. Oakland Athletics, St. Louis Cardinals
    d. Oakland Athletics, Texas Rangers

20. In 1989, the Yankees acquired Jesse Barfield from the

Toronto Blue Jays for which former player and current MLB Network analyst?

a. Kevin Millar
b. Al Leiter
c. Ron Darling
d. Eric Byrnes

QUIZ ANSWERS

1. A- Curse of the Bambino

2. B- Roger Clemens

3. C- Alex Rodriguez

4. B – Curtis Granderson

5. D- David Justice

6. B- Chicago White Sox

7. A- Giancarlo Stanton

8. D- Kansas City Athletics

9. A – 5

10. A- True

11. C- 15 trades

12. A – True

13. B- Ichiro Suzuki

14. A- True

15. B- False

16. C- Chase Headley

17. C – San Francisco Giants

18. A- California Angels

19. C- Oakland Athletics, St. Louis Cardinals

20. B – Al Leiter

DID YOU KNOW?

1. The New York Yankees are often touted as being successful because of the fact that they have "the biggest payroll in baseball". Yet in reality, the Yankees have not had the biggest payroll in baseball since 2012.

2. The Yankees have made trades with all 30 current MLB teams. Yes, even the Red Sox.

3. The "Curse of the Bambino" trade is widely considered the best Yankees trade of all time. Unless you're a Red Sox fans, then it was considered the worst. This trade involved the Red Sox selling Babe Ruth to the Yankees to fund Broadway plays.

4. Trading Fred McGriff is widely considered the worst Yankees trade of all time. He hit 493 home runs in his career, but none of those were with the Yanks. The Yanks went with Don Mattingly at first base instead.

5. Current Yankees General Manager, Brian Cashman began working for the Yankees in 1986 as a college intern. He became Assistant GM in 1992 and became General Manager in 1998.

6. In 2001, the Yankees traded David Justice to the New York Mets for Robin Ventura. A week later, David Justice was traded to the A's. Because of this, he was featured in the book and movie, *Moneyball*.

7. Current Yanks slugger, Giancarlo Stanton formerly went by the name "Mike Stanton" (not to be confused with former Yanks relief pitcher, Mike Stanton) when he debuted with the Florida Marlins. His full name is Giancarlo Cruz Michael Stanton.

8. In 1976, the Yankees purchased pitcher, Vida Blue from the Oakland A's. In his career, Blue won a Cy Young Award and American League MVP.

9. In 1986, the Yankees traded Don Baylor to the Boston Red Sox. It was the only trade the Yanks and Red Sox made in the '80s.

10. The New York Yankees and New York Mets have made 14 trades total since their first trade in 1966.

CHAPTER 8:

DRAFT DAY

QUIZ TIME!

1. With the ___ overall pick in first round of the 1992 MLB draft, the New York Yankees selected SS Derek Jeter.

    a. 1st
    b. 2nd
    c. 6th
    d. 10th

2. With the 32nd overall pick in first round of the 2013 MLB draft, the New York Yankees selected OF Aaron Judge. The pick the Yanks used to draft Judge was received as compensation after losing Nick Swisher in free agency to the Cleveland Indians.

    a. True
    b. False

3. The Yankees lost their 2002 first round draft pick to the Oakland A's as compensation for signing which free agent?

    a. David Justice

b. Nick Swisher

c. Johnny Damon

d. Jason Giambi

4. Which pitcher was chosen by the Yankees 41st overall in the 2006 MLB Draft? He made his debut with New York the following season.

   a. Phil Hughes

   b. Joba Chamberlain

   c. Ian Kennedy

   d. Gerrit Cole

5. Which former Yankees captain was drafted 4th overall in 1968? He was the 1970 American League Rookie of the Year, won an American League MVP Award in 1976 and appeared in seven All-Star Games in a span of eight years.

   a. Willie Randolph

   b. Graig Nettles

   c. Don Mattingly

   d. Thurmon Munson

6. The Yankees 2019 First-Round draft pick, SS Anthony Volpe, like Derek Jeter, was drafted out of high school.

   a. True

   b. False

7. In the 2017 MLB Draft, The Yankees 40 draft picks came from 40 different schools.

   a. True

   b. False

8. With the ___ overall pick in ____round of the 1979 MLB draft, the New York Yankees selected 1B Don Mattingly.

    a. 3rd, 1st
    b. 103rd, 4th
    c. 493rd, 19th
    d. 680th, 27th

9. In the 1990 MLB Draft, C Jorge Posada was selected by the Yankees in the 24th round (646th overall). Where was he drafted out of?

    a. Alejandrino High School
    b. Calhoun Community College
    c. Wallace State Community College
    d. The University of Alabama

10. Bo Jackson was drafted by the Yankees out of high school but decided to attend Auburn University instead.

    a. True
    b. False

11. Which current Yankees outfielder was drafted 109th overall in the third round by the Yankees in the 2005 draft?

    a. Brett Gardner
    b. Mike Tauchman
    c. Aaron Hicks
    d. Clint Fraizer

12. Ian Kennedy was drafted in 2006 by the Yankees in the first round, 21st overall. He played 41 games for the Yankees over the course of 3 seasons.

a. True

b. False

13. With the 23rd overall pick in first round of the 2004 MLB draft, the New York Yankees selected pitcher, _____.

a. Tyler Clippard

b. Phil Hughes

c. Ross Ohlendorf

d. Mike Mussina

14. In the ____ round of the 2006 MLB draft, the New York Yankees selected pitcher, David Robertson.

a. 2nd

b. 43rd

c. 20th

d. 17th

15. In the ____ round of the 1990 MLB draft, the New York Yankees selected pitcher, Andy Pettitte.

a. 2nd

b. 22nd

c. 12th

d. 21st

16. In the ____ round of the 1990 MLB draft, the New York Yankees selected OF Carl Everett ____ overall.

a. 4th, 110th

b. 3rd, 94th

c. 1st, 1st

d. 1st, 10th

17. In 1970, the Yankees drafted pitcher, Dave Cheadle in the first round. He only pitched 4 games in his entire career, all with the Atlanta Braves. His career ERA is 18.00 with a record of 0-1.

    a. 0
    b. 2
    c. 6
    d. 24

18. Which Baltimore Orioles player was drafted by the Yankees in 2004, but did not sign?

    a. Mark Trumbo
    b. Pedro Severino
    c. Chris Davis
    d. Aaron Brooks

19. Which Los Angeles Dodgers player was drafted by the Yankees in 2005, but did not sign?

    a. Justin Turner
    b. Cory Seager
    c. Joc Pederson
    d. Cody Bellinger

20. In the 8th round of the 2005 MLB draft, the Yankees selected OF Austin Jackson.

    a. True
    b. False

QUIZ ANSWERS

1. C – 6th

2. A – True

3. D – Jason Giambi

4. B- Joba Chamberlain

5. D- Thurmon Munson

6. A- True, He passed up a college commitment to Vanderbilt

7. A- True

8. C – 493rd, 19th

9. B- Calhoun Community College

10. A- True

11. A- Brett Gardner

12. B- False, He played 14 games for the Yankees over the course of 3 seasons

13. B – Phil Hughes

14. D – 17th

15. B- 22nd

16. D- 1st, 10th

17. A – 0

18. C – Chris Davis

19. A- Justin Turner

20. A- True

DID YOU KNOW?

1. In 2008, the Yankees drafted pitcher Gerrit Cole 28th overall. No offer was made, because Cole decided to honor his commitment to attend UCLA. He was then drafted by the Pittsburgh Pirates, 1st overall in 2011. Now in 2020, things have come full circle and he is once again a member of the Yankees.

2. The Yankees drafted C Jorge Posada in 1989, but he decided to not sign and stay at his community college instead. They drafted him again, a year later and he then signed. He did not attend a 4-year university, because his SAT scores were too low in high school.

3. Former Yankee, Dave Winfield was drafted out of college by four different teams in three different pro sports including the San Diego Padres (MLB), Atlanta Hawks (NBA), Utah Stars (ABA) and Minnesota Vikings (NFL).

4. When the Yankees signed 1B Mark Teixeira, the Anaheim Angels received a compensation pick, which they used to draft star outfielder, Mike Trout.

5. Aaron Judge was drafted by the Oakland A's in 2010 out of high school, but he decided to attend college in Fresno instead. He was then drafted by the Yanks in 2013.

6. The MLB draft was implemented because teams used to be able to sign players by simply offering them a contract.

Due to this, wealthier teams, like the Yankees were able to stockpile stars and poorer teams suffered.

7. Deion Sanders played in both the NFL and the MLB. He was drafted by the Yankees in 1988. He played in 71 games for the Yankees from 1989-1990. He is the only person in history to win both a World Series and a Super Bowl.

8. In 1970, the Yankees drafted pitcher, Dave Cheadle in the first round. He only pitched 4 games in his entire career, all with the Atlanta Braves. His career ERA is 18.00 with a record of 0-1.

9. The Yankees have only ever had two No. 1 overall selections in the MLB Draft in franchise history. The first was in 1967, they chose a first baseman named Ron Blomberg. The second was in 1991, they chose a pitcher named Brien Taylor.

10. Former NFL Quarterback, John Elway was drafted by the Yankees with the final pick in the second round in 1981, six picks before San Diego Padres Hall of Famer Tony Gwynn.

CHAPTER 9:

ODDS & ENDS

QUIZ TIME!

1. While in college, former Yankee outfielder, Dave Winfield was arrested for stealing a _____.

    a. Snowblower

    b. Bag of Chips

    c. Baseball Glove

    d. Lawn Mower

2. Former Yankee, Jose Canseco has a twin brother who also played in the MLB.

    a. True

    b. False

3. Former Yankee, Nick Swisher is married to which Hollywood actress?

    a. Hillary Duff

    b. Joanna Garcia

    c. Lea Michele

    d. Anna Kendrick

4. Earle Combs was a _____ before he was a baseball player. He decided to switch careers when he realized he could make more money playing baseball.

    a. Schoolteacher
    b. Coal Miner
    c. Doctor
    d. Journalist

5. In a high school football game, former Yankee Johnny Damon suffered his first sports concussion at the hands of which NFL star?

    a. Ronnie Lott
    b. Michael Strahan
    c. Troy Polamalu
    d. Warren Sapp

6. Joe DiMaggio was married to which famous actress?

    a. Marilyn Monroe
    b. Lucille Ball
    c. Katharine Hepburn
    d. Judy Garland

7. When he was a little kid in Panama, Mariano Rivera played baseball with milk cartons, fishing nets and tree branches.

    a. True
    b. False

8. Whitey Ford's MLB career was interrupted for two-years by what?

    a. A break to care for his elderly parents

b. A stint in the U.S. Army

c. A break to spend time with his children

d. A stint pitching for a team in Japan

9. Which former Yankee coached the American League in the 2010 'Taco Bell All-Star Legends & Celebrity Softball Game'?

    a. Rickey Henderson

    b. Reggie Jackson

    c. Roger Clemens

    d. Goose Gossage

10. How many times was Billy Martin hired and fired as Yankees manager?

    a. 2

    b. 3

    c. 4

    d. 5

11. In 2018, which former Yankees pitcher became a pitching coach for a high school team alongside Lance Berkman, the team's head coach and former MLB star?

    a. Mariano Rivera

    b. Randy Johnson

    c. Andy Pettitte

    d. Joba Chamberlain

12. The illness that killed Lou Gehrig, ALS, is commonly referred to as Lou Gehrig's Disease.

    a. True

    b. False

13. Former Yankee Don Mattingly took over for former Yankees manager, Joe Torre as manager for which MLB team in 2011?

    a. San Diego Padres
    b. Los Angeles Dodgers
    c. Houston Astros
    d. Seattle Mariners

14. Which former Yankee was the first athlete to appear on a box of Wheaties?

    a. Babe Ruth
    b. Joe DiMaggio
    c. Lou Gehrig
    d. Mickey Mantle

15. How many days did Babe Ruth's body lay open casket in Yankee Stadium for fans to pay their respects?

    a. 2
    b. 1
    c. 3
    d. 7

16. Joe DiMaggio made the All-Star team every season in his MLB career.

    a. True
    b. False

17. In 1960, Yankees owner George Steinbrenner bought a basketball team called the:

    a. New York Squirrels

b. San Francisco Seagulls

c. Cleveland Pipers

d. Dallas Hummingbirds

18. In which city does the Yankees Triple-A team play?

a. Scranton, Pennsylvania

b. Providence, Rhode Island

c. Hartford, Connecticut

d. Long Island, New York

19. Former Yankee, Tony Lazzeri's parents immigrated from
_____ to San Francisco.

a. Spain

b. Italy

c. Mexico

d. France

20. Former Yankees manager, Billy Martin ironically died
after suffering from Lou Gehrig's Disease (ALS).

a. True

b. False

QUIZ ANSWERS

1. A- Snowblower

2. A – True

3. B- Joanna Garcia

4. A- Schoolteacher

5. D- Warren Sapp

6. A- Marilyn Monroe

7. A – True

8. B – A stint in the U.S. Army

9. D – Goose Gossage

10. D- 5

11. C- Andy Pettitte

12. A – True

13. B- Los Angeles Dodgers

14. C – Lou Gehrig

15. A- 2

16. A – True

17. C- Cleveland Pipers

18. A- Scranton, Pennsylvania

19. B- Italy

20. B – False, He died in a car accident on Christmas Day

DID YOU KNOW?

1. At one point in his life, Babe Ruth lived on the site that is now Camden Yards, home of the Baltimore Orioles.

2. After his retirement from baseball, Bob Meusel worked as a security guard at a U.S. Navy base for 15 years. He also played himself in two baseball films, Pride of the Yankees and The Babe Ruth Story.

3. Current Yankee, Aaron Judge was adopted the day after he was born by his mom Patti and dad Wayne, both schoolteachers from California.

4. Back in 1998, former Yankee Alex Rodriguez was asked by a reporter who his dream date would be with. His answer? Jennifer Lopez. 22 years later, J-Lo and A-Rod are currently engaged to be married.

5. Former Yankee, Robinson Cano was named after Jackie Robinson. His dad, Jose briefly played for the Houston Astros and always pitches to his son when he is in the MLB Home Run Derby.

6. Thurmon Munson was the first Yankees Captain after the legendary Lou Gehrig. After Munson came Graig Nettles, Willie Randloph, Ron Guidry, Don Mattingly, and of course, Derek Jeter.

7. Before the last game at Old Yankee Stadium, Jorge Posada caught a ceremonial first pitch from Julia Ruth, Babe Ruth's last surviving daughter at the time.

8. Yogi Berra once sued Hanna-Barbera for defamation over their character, Yogi Bear. He later withdrew the lawsuit.

9. Casey Stengel was known for his misuse of the English language. The way he talked was nicknamed "Stengelese".

10. In 2005, former Yankees manager, Joe Torre carried the Olympic Torch in Florence, Italy, running it 405 meters to the famous Ponte Vecchio bridge.

CHAPTER 10:

OUTFIELDERS

QUIZ TIME!

1. Which team has former Yankee outfielder; Curtis Granderson NOT played for?

    a. Los Angeles Dodgers

    b. New York Mets

    c. Detroit Tigers

    d. Texas Rangers

2. Current Yankee, Giancarlo Stanton's first MLB home run was a grand slam, only 32 at-bats into his career.

    a. True

    b. False

3. In what year was Reggie Jackson elected to the National Baseball Hall of Fame?

    a. 1999

    b. 1995

    c. 1993

    d. 1997

4. Paul O'Neill is the only player in MLB history to have played on the winning team in three perfect games.

    a. True
    b. False

5. Which of these teams did former Yankee outfielder, Lou Piniella NOT manage in his coaching career?

    a. Tampa Bay Devil Rays
    b. Los Angeles Dodgers
    c. Chicago Cubs
    d. New York Yankees

6. Before moving to outfield, what position did Babe Ruth play in 127 appearances?

    a. Pitcher
    b. First Baseman
    c. Catcher
    d. Second Baseman

7. Bernie Williams played his entire 16- year career with the Yankees.

    a. True
    b. False

8. How many seasons did Raúl Ibañez play for the Yankees?

    a. 3
    b. 2
    c. 1
    d. He was never a Yankee

9. Roger Maris played in _____ World Series in the 60's; more than any other player.

   a. 4
   b. 10
   c. 5
   d. 7

10. Gary Sheffield is the nephew of which former MLB star pitcher?

    a. Dave Stewart
    b. Dwight Gooden
    c. Sandy Koufax
    d. Gaylord Perry

11. Which former Yankee is one of only two players in the MLB to reach the World Series in three consecutive years with three different teams?

    a. Carlos Beltran
    b. Joe Pepitone
    c. Don Baylor
    d. Ichiro Suzuki

12. Bobby Murcer played a combined 1,881 games in 15 seasons, all with the Yankees.

    a. True
    b. False

13. Joe DiMaggio received the Presidential Medal of Freedom from which former U.S. president?

    a. Ronald Reagan

b. Harry Truman

c. Gerald Ford

d. Barack Obama

14. Comedian Billy Crystal outbid former Yankee, David Wells for which famous Yankees outfielder's used baseball gloves? He paid $239,000.

a. Joe DiMaggio

b. Babe Ruth

c. Roger Maris

d. Mickey Mantle

15. Which Yankee was the first Japanese player to hit 100 home runs in the MLB?

a. Ichiro Suzuki

b. Masahiro Tanaka

c. Hideki Matsui

d. Hiroki Kuroda

16. Aaron Judge was the first rookie in history to win the MLB Home Run Derby.

a. True

b. False

17. Which former Yankees outfielder was the first member of the Navajo Nation to play in the MLB?

a. Gene Locklear

b. Zack Wheat

c. Louis Sockalexis

d. Jacoby Ellsbury

18. Former Yankee, Chili Davis has been the hitting coach for which two MLB teams?

    a. San Francisco Giants and New York Mets
    b. Oakland A's and New York Mets
    c. Oakland A's and Minnesota Twins
    d. Minnesota Twins and San Francisco Giants

19. Which former Yankees outfielder became the first rookie in MLB history to hit two home runs in a World Series game?

    a. Charlie Keller
    b. Roy White
    c. Aaron Judge
    d. Brett Gardner

20. Mickey Mantle holds the World Series record for the longest hitting streak at 17 games.

    a. True
    b. False

QUIZ ANSWERS

1. D – Texas Rangers

2. A – True

3. C – 1993

4. A- True

5. B- Los Angeles Dodgers

6. A- Pitcher

7. A – True

8. C – 1

9. D – 7

10. B – Dwight Gooden

11. C- Don Baylor

12. B- False, Ron White

13. C- Gerald Ford

14. D- Mickey Mantle

15. C- Hideki Matsui

16. A – True

17. D – Jacoby Ellsbury

18. B- Oakland A's and New York Mets

19. A- Charlie Keller

20. B – False, Hank Bauer

DID YOU KNOW?

1. Joe DiMaggio missed being teammates with Babe Ruth by two seasons. He was teammates with Lou Gehrig for four seasons.

2. Since retirement, Johnny Damon has starred on several reality shows including Celebrity Apprentice, Dancing with the Stars, and Below Deck.

3. Bernie Williams is a classically trained guitarist. Since his retirement from baseball, he has released two jazz albums and was nominated for a Latin Grammy.

4. Aaron Judge is incredibly tall. At 6 ft, 7 in, he is the 11th tallest player in MLB history.

5. In a 1983 exhibition game against the Toronto Blue Jays, Dave Winfield threw a baseball that struck and killed a seagull when he was warming up in-between innings. He was arrested by Toronto Police on animal cruelty charges. The charges were quickly dropped the following day.

6. Yankees outfielder, Giancarlo Stanton was offered football scholarships from both UCLA and UNLV. He instead was drafted by the Marlins out of high school, and he decided to not attend college and instead play professional baseball.

7. Babe Ruth never wore the Yankees famous 'NY' interlocking logo. It did not become a permanent part of the Yanks uniform until two years after Ruth left.

8. Mickey Mantle suffered from anxiety attacks and alcoholism. In the mornings he would drink what he called the "Breakfast of Champions"- a shot of brandy with Kahlua and cream.

9. Roger Maris' single-season MLB record 61 home runs stood for 37 years until Mark McGwire hit 70 in 1998.

10. After retirement, Reggie Jackson worked for Upper Deck, the baseball card company. He also starred in the movie, *Benchwarmers*, starring Rob Schneider, David Spade, Jon Heder, and Jon Lovitz. Everyone remembers that scene where he smashed mailboxes with a bat, right?

CHAPTER 11:

INFIELDERS

QUIZ TIME!

1. Which former Yankee holds the All-Time Grand Slam Record?

    a. Derek Jeter
    b. Alex Rodriguez
    c. Babe Ruth
    d. Mickey Mantle

2. A benign tumor shortened 1B Jason Giambi's 2004 season.

    a. True
    b. False

3. Lou Gehrig's record for consecutive games played was surpassed by which MLB star in 1995?

    a. Cal Ripken Jr.
    b. Mark McGwire
    c. Mike Piazza
    d. Ken Griffey Jr.

4. What does the 'DJ' stand for in DJ LaMahieu's name?

a. Doug Jr.
b. Dakota Jr.
c. Daniel James
d. David John

5. Which former Yankee 1st baseman holds the all-time MLB record for most games with a home run from both sides of the plate?

   a. Tino Martinez
   b. Don Mattingly
   c. Mark Teixeira
   d. Lou Gehrig

6. Which former Yankees 2nd baseman was the first MLB player to hit two grand slams during the same game?

   a. Willie Randolph
   b. Tony Lazzeri
   c. Joe Gordon
   d. Snuffy Stirnweiss

7. Luke Voit was hit by a pitch in his first MLB plate appearance.

   a. True
   b. False

8. Which former Yankee is the only MLB player to be named World Series MVP, despite them being on the losing team?

   a. Derek Jeter
   b. Billy Martin
   c. Bobby Richardson
   d. Robinson Cano

9. During _____'s entire career with the Yankees, they won the AL Pennant every year and the World Series three years in a row.

    a. Red Rolfe
    b. Jason Giambi
    c. Joe Gordon
    d. Scott Brosius

10. How many games did Troy Tulowitzki play in for the Yanks in 2019?

    a. 29
    b. 5
    c. 88
    d. 75

11. Didi Gregorius goes by the nickname "Didi" because his U.S. teammates could never understand how to pronounce his given first name. What is his real first name?

    a. Mariekson
    b. Jovian
    c. Hasani
    d. Severus

12. Former Yankee, Starlin Castro was the first MLB player who was born in the 1990's.

    a. True
    b. False

13. Which former Yankee broke up current Yankee, CC Sabathia's perfect game bid in the seventh inning in 2011?

a. Mark Teixeria

b. Brendan Ryan

c. Jason Giambi

d. Stephen Drew

14. Which Yankees shortstop was named World Series MVP in 1978?

a. Phil Rizzuto

b. Bobby Meacham

c. Bucky Dent

d. Tony Kubek

15. Which former Yankees shortstop, other than Derek Jeter, wore the Number 2?

a. Frankie Crosetti

b. Mark Koenig

c. Both of the Above

d. None of the Above

16. Former Yankee Tom Tresh was the son of former MLB catcher, Mike Tresh

a. True

b. False

17. After his playing career with the Yankees, Red Rolfe went on to manage what MLB team from 1949-1952?

a. Boston Braves

b. St. Louis Browns

c. Pittsburgh Pirates

d. Detroit Tigers

18. Chase Headley only played for the Yankees and one other team in his MLB career. Who was the other team he played for?

    a. Texas Rangers
    b. Miami Marlins
    c. San Diego Padres
    d. Seattle Mariners

19. Which former Yankee won the 1942 AL MVP?

    a. Mickey Mantle
    b. Gil McDougald
    c. Joe Gordon
    d. Tony Lazzeri

20. Alex Rodriguez won three World Series with the Yankees.

    a. True
    b. False

QUIZ ANSWERS

1. B – Alex Rodriguez

2. A – True

3. A- Cal Ripken Jr.

4. D – David John

5. C- Mark Teixeira

6. B – Tony Lazzeri

7. A – True

8. C- Bobby Richardson

9. D- Scott Brosius

10. B- 5

11. A- Mariekson

12. A- True

13. B- Brendan Ryan

14. C- Bucky Dent

15. C – Both of the Above

16. A- True

17. D- Detroit Tigers

18. C – San Diego Padres

19. C – Joe Gordon

20. B- False, One

DID YOU KNOW?

1. After his career playing shortstop for the Yankees, Phil Rizzuto spent 40 years as a Yankees radio and TV announcer. His trademark saying during broadcasts was "Holy cow!"

2. Roger Peckinpaugh was only 23 years old when he temporarily managed the Yankees in 1914. He was Babe Ruth's choice to manage the Yanks again in 1922.

3. Bucky Dent was the first shortstop to ever win World Series MVP in MLB history.

4. Kevin Youkilis was a Yankee enemy for years when he was a Red Sox star. He then played the final season of his career in New York as a Yankee. He now owns Loma Brewing Company in Northern California.

5. 3B Eric Chavez played for the Oakland A's for 12 seasons until being traded to the Yankees in 2011. In retirement, he has been a color analyst and play by play announcer for A's broadcasts, served as special assistant to Brian Cashman with the Yankees, been a special assistant for the LA Angels, and is now manager of the minor league Salt Lake Bees.

6. Former Yankee, Todd Frazier was a Little League World Series hero in 1998. At only 12-years old, he batted .600 overall and was 4 for 4 with a leadoff home run in the

championship game. His Toms River East All- Stars beat Japan for the title.

7. Don Mattingly is the only Yankee to have his number retired without having won a World Series with the franchise. His time with the Yanks marked the longest drought of reaching the World Series. Mattingly went on to manage the Los Angeles Dodgers and currently, the Miami Marlins. He credits Tony LaRussa as being his managerial idol.

8. The one year waiting period to be elected to the National Baseball Hall of Fame was waived for Lou Gehrig. He entered the Hall in late 1939.

9. Both Jason Giambi and his brother, Jeremy Giambi played in the MLB. Jason had a much more successful career though.

10. Derek Jeter won a lot of awards in his career to say the least. Some include: AL Rookie of the Year (1996), World Series MVP (2000), 5 Gold Glove Awards, 5 Silver Slugger Awards, 2 AL Hank Aaron Awards, and the Roberto Clemente Award (2004).

CHAPTER 12:

PITCHERS AND CATCHERS

QUIZ TIME!

1. Where was CC Sabathia born?

    a. Vallejo, California

    b. Vacaville, California

    c. San Diego, California

    d. Napa, California

2. In 1978, Ron Guidry had a 25-3 record on the season, which led to his AL Cy Young Award win.

    a. True

    b. False

3. Gary Sanchez is the fastest catcher in MLB history to reach ___ home runs.

    a. 25

    b. 50

    c. 100

    d. 300

4. Which former Yankees manager was never a catcher in their playing career?

    a. Joe Girardi

    b. Joe Torre

    c. Yogi Berra

    d. Aaron Boone

5. Which former Yanks pitcher has a common baseball surgery named after them?

    a. Luis Severino

    b. Tommy John

    c. J.A. Happ

    d. Spud Chandler

6. Which Yankees pitcher holds the record for fastest pitch ever thrown, at 105.1 mph?

    a. Andy Pettitte

    b. Aroldis Chapman

    c. Mariano Rivera

    d. Red Ruffing

7. Lefty Gomez was Walt Disney's 3rd cousin.

    a. True

    b. False

8. Which former Yankee was the first American League relief pitcher to win the Cy Young Award?

    a. Goose Gossage

    b. Whitey Ford

    c. Waite Hoyt

    d. Sparky Lyle

9. Which former Yankees catcher was the first catcher to win the American League Rookie of the Year Award?

   a. Jorge Posada
   b. Yogi Berra
   c. Thurmon Munson
   d. Bill Dickey

10. Derek Jeter hired which former Yankees catcher as a special adviser to the Miami Marlins' front office?

   a. Brian McCann
   b. Jorge Posada
   c. Russell Martin
   d. Joe Girardi

11. Nolan Ryan and former Yankee, _____ are the only two pitchers in MLB history to throw a no-hitter after their 40th birthday. _____ is also the only 40-plus year old to throw a perfect game in MLB history.

   a. Andy Pettitte
   b. Goose Gossage
   c. CC Sabathia
   d. Randy Johnson

12. Former Yankee pitcher, Catfish Hunter died from Lou Gehrig's disease, the disease named after another former Yankee.

   a. True
   b. False

13. Which former Yankees pitcher ended his career with the

highest winning percentage by a player with at least 100 wins in MLB history, at .717?

    a. Spud Chandler

    b. Mel Stottlemyre

    c. Bob Shawkey

    d. Vic Raschi

14. Former Yankees pitcher, Dave Righetti served as pitching coach from 2000-2017 for which MLB team?

    a. Tampa Bay Rays

    b. Texas Rangers

    c. San Francisco Giants

    d. Milwaukee Brewers

15. On June 17, 1978, which former Yankees pitcher struck out 18 total California Angels players in one game, a Yanks team record that still stands today?

    a. Ed Figueroa

    b. Ron Guidry

    c. Catfish Hunter

    d. Goose Gossage

16. In 1965, Mel Stottlemyer hit an inside-the-park grand slam. No Yankee pitcher since has ever hit a inside-the-park grand slam.

    a. True

    b. False

17. On May 17, 1998 _____ pitched the 15th perfect game in MLB history and the 2nd perfect game in Yankees history.

a. David Cone

b. Andy Pettitte

c. Mike Stanton

d. David Wells

18. Which Yankees catcher broke the color barrier for the Yankees in 1955? Many dubbed him the Jackie Robinson of the pinstripes.

a. Jesse Gonder

b. Elston Howard

c. Moses Fleetwood Walker

d. Elrod Hendricks

19. Which former Yankee was the first MLB pitcher to throw a perfect game in the World Series?

a. Don Larsen

b. Whitey Ford

c. Joba Chamberlain

d. Mike Mussina

20. Former Yankees catcher, Wally Schang was the first pitcher in MLB history to hit a home run from both sides of the plate in the same game.

a. True

b. False

QUIZ ANSWERS

1. A- Vallejo, California

2. A- True

3. C- 100

4. D- Aaron Boone

5. B- Tommy John

6. B – Aroldis Chapman

7. B- False

8. D – Sparky Lyle

9. C- Thurmon Munson

10. B – Jorge Posada

11. D – Randy Johnson

12. A – True

13. A- Spud Chandler

14. C- San Francisco Giants

15. B- Ron Guidry

16. A- True

17. D – David Wells

18. B – Elston Howard

19. A – Don Larsen

20. A – True

DID YOU KNOW?

1. Andy Pettitte is the only MLB pitcher who played at least 18 seasons without ever having a losing record on the season. He also won the most games of any MLB pitcher in the 2000s.

2. Only 11 players in MLB history have a palindrome (spelled same backwards and forwards) for a last name. Former Yankee catcher, Truck Hannah is one of them. 'Hannah' is spelled the same both backwards and forwards.

3. Once former Yankees pitcher, Ralph Terry retired from baseball, he became a professional golfer. He is the only former MLB player to win a PGA Tour event.

4. Jack Chesbro was the first starting pitcher in the first game for the New York Highlanders.

5. Pitcher Vic Raschi won 21 games in three consecutive seasons. He is the only Yankees player to ever win back-to-back-to-back 20-win seasons.

6. Former Yankees pitcher, Herb Pennock wrote the famous "10 Commandments for Pitchers". You can view the commandments on Baseball Almanac's website.

7. Former Yankees, Randy Johnson, Al Leiter, Derek Lowe, Terry Mulholland, Kevin Brown, and A.J. Burnett each have at least one win against all 30 MLB teams. Only 18 MLB pitchers have done this in their careers.

8. In 1967, former Yankees pitcher, Al Downing was the first Yankee in history to record a perfect, immaculate inning. 9 pitches- 9 strikes- 3 outs.

9. In the first game ever played at the original Yankee Stadium, Bob Shawkey was the starting pitcher and the Yanks won.

10. Mariano Rivera was the first pitcher to make 1,000 game appearances with the same team in MLB history.

CHAPTER 13:

27 RINGS

QUIZ TIME!

1. Who was the 2009 World Series MVP?

    a. Derek Jeter
    b. Hideki Matsui
    c. Nick Swisher
    d. Mariano Rivera

2. The Yankees have won nine more World Series titles than any other MLB team has made World Series appearances.

    a. True
    b. False

3. Which two Yankees managers are tied for most World Series wins as manager?

    a. Joe Torre and Yogi Berra
    b. Joe Torre and Joe McCarthy
    c. Casey Stengel and Billy Martin
    d. Casey Stengel and Joe McCarthy

4. Since their first World Series appearance in 1921, the Yankees have won at least two World Series titles every decade except in the _____ and _____.

   a. 1950's and 1990's
   b. 1960's and 2000's
   c. 1980's and 2010's
   d. 1930's and 1970's

5. How many innings did Whitey Ford pitch in the World Series in his career?

   a. 100
   b. 146
   c. 81
   d. 49

6. How many times have the Bronx Bombers reached the World Series in MLB history?

   a. 50
   b. 44
   c. 30
   d. 40

7. The Yankees were the first MLB team to win World Series' in the first and the last years of the decade.

   a. True
   b. False

8. Which player hit the first World Series home run at the original Yankee Stadium?

   a. Babe Ruth

b. Casey Stengel

c. Irish Meusel

d. Bullet Joe Bush

9. In what year did the Yankees win their first World Series Championship?

   a. 1923

   b. 1925

   c. 1927

   d. 1929

10. Who did the Yankees defeat in the 2000 World Series?

    a. New York Mets

    b. Florida Marlins

    c. Montreal Expos

    d. Philadelphia Phillies

11. Who was the Yankees manager during their 1978 World Series win?

    a. Dick Howser

    b. Billy Martin

    c. Bob Lemon

    d. Bucky Dent

12. The 2009 World Series was the first in MLB history to have regularly scheduled games in November.

    a. True

    b. False

13. Who did the Yankees defeat in the 1962 World Series?

    a. Cincinnati Reds

b. St. Louis Cardinals

c. Chicago Cubs

d. San Francisco Giants

14. What year was the Yankees last Subway Series World Series against the New York Giants?

   a. 1956

   b. 1951

   c. 1952

   d. 1949

15. Which former Yankee won the 1996 World Series MVP?

   a. Derek Jeter

   b. Darryl Strawberry

   c. John Wetteland

   d. Bernie Williams

16. The Boston Celtics of the NBA have more championships than the Yankees.

   a. True

   b. False

17. Who was the starting pitcher for Game 4 in the 1999 World Series?

   a. Orlando Hernandez

   b. David Cone

   c. Andy Pettitte

   d. Roger Clemens

18. During which World Series did Reggie Jackson earn his nickname, "Mr. October"?

a. 1977

b. 1962

c. 1978

d. 1958

19. Which player was the 1956 World Series MVP?

    a. Yogi Berra

    b. Don Larsen

    c. Mickey Mantle

    d. Hank Bauer

20. The Yankees won the last all-white World Series before integration.

    a. True

    b. False

QUIZ ANSWERS

1. B – Hideki Matsui

2. A – True

3. D- Casey Stengel and Joe McCarthy

4. C- 1980's and 2010's

5. B – 146

6. D- 40

7. A – True

8. B- Casey Stengel

9. A- 1923

10. A- New York Mets

11. C- Bob Lemon

12. A – True

13. D- San Francisco Giants

14. B- 1951

15. C – John Wetteland

16. B- False, the Celtics have 17 championships

17. D – Roger Clemens

18. A – 1977

19. B- Don Larsen

20. A- True

DID YOU KNOW?

1. The Yankees have the most championships of any MLB team. They have more than twice the number of championships of the second ranked, St. Louis Cardinals. They also have three times more World Series wins compared to their rival, the Boston Red Sox.

2. Whitey Ford holds the record for consecutive World Series innings pitched with 33. Babe Ruth previously held the record with 29 2/3.

3. Yogi Berra was the first player in MLB history to hit a pinch-hit home run in the World Series.

4. Many believe the Yankees were cheated out of reaching the 2019 World Series against the Washington Nationals. The Houston Astros were found to have cheated during the season. The Astros defeated the Yankees in the ALCS to move on to the World Series. CC Sabathia and Aaron Judge both have voiced their opinions about this situation.

5. The Yankees won 6 World Series in the 1950s. Three of those championships were won against the Brooklyn Dodgers.

6. Yankee Hall of Famers, Derek Jeter and Mariano Rivera won one World Series MVP each. Rivera in 1999, Jeter in 2000.

7. Yogi Berra won the most World Series as a player in MLB history with 10 total.

8. Mariano Rivera pitched in the most World Series games in MLB history. He passed Whitey Ford's record in the 2009 World Series.

9. Joe Girardi, Billy Martin, and Ralph Houk are the only Yankees to win the World Series both as a Yankees player and a Yankees manager.

10. The 1999 Yankees only lost one game during the playoffs.

CHAPTER 14:

THE HEATED RIVALRIES

QUIZ TIME!

1. How many times have the Yankees and Dodgers played each other in the World Series?

    a. 9 times
    b. 5 times
    c. 11 times
    d. 12 times

2. The Yankees have only met the Red Sox once in the American League Division Series (ALDS), in 2018.

    a. True
    b. False

3. The Red Sox broke the 'Curse of the Bambino' by winning the World Series in which year?

    a. 2001
    b. 2004
    c. 2005
    d. 2007

4. In 2019, the Yankees and Red Sox played the first regular season MLB game in what famous international city?

   a. Paris
   b. Barcelona
   c. London
   d. Dublin

5. In the first 100 years of the Yankees-Red Sox rivalry, how many times did they face each other in the World Series?

   a. 3
   b. 22
   c. 11
   d. 0

6. In the 2004 ALCS, the Red Sox beat the Yankees in 7 games. Who won ALCS MVP?

   a. Johnny Damon
   b. David Ortiz
   c. Manny Ramirez
   d. Pedro Martinez

7. The Highlanders and NY Giants briefly shared Hilltop Park, which was a big part of their rivalry.

   a. True
   b. False

8. Which Yankee pitcher threw a no-hitter against the Red Sox on the 4th of July in 1983?

   a. Goose Gossage
   b. Matt Keough

c. Ron Guidry

d. Dave Righetti

9. When did the regular season Subway Series between the Yankees and New York Mets begin?

   a. 1969

   b. 1988

   c. 1997

   d. 2001

10. How many times have the Yankees and Mets met in the World Series?

    a. 0

    b. 1

    c. 5

    d. 11

11. Which team was never a part of a Subway Series with the Yankees?

    a. Mets

    b. Giants

    c. Athletics

    d. Dodgers

12. No player in MLB history has won a World Series with both the Yankees and the Red Sox.

    a. True

    b. False

13. Which player has NOT played for both the Yankees and the Mets?

a. Robinson Cano

b. Darryl Strawberry

c. Bernie Williams

d. Yogi Berra

14. Which player has NOT played for both the Yankees and the Red Sox?

    a. Johnny Damon

    b. Wade Boggs

    c. Jason Giambi

    d. Babe Ruth

15. What is the name of the Red Sox owner who sold Babe Ruth to the Yankees in 1920?

    a. Tom Yawkey

    b. Bob Quinn

    c. Charles Somers

    d. Harry Frazee

16. The New York Highlanders played the Red Sox in the first game ever played at Fenway Park in 1912.

    a. True

    b. False

17. Which pitcher threw the first no-hitter between the Highlanders and Red Sox in 1908?

    a. Eddie Cicotte

    b. Cy Young

    c. Jack Chesbro

    d. Joe Lake

18. How many times did the Yanks and the NY Giants face each other in the World Series?

    a. 3 times
    b. 6 times
    c. 1 time
    d. 10 times

19. Which former Yankees manager has also been manager for the Red Sox?

    a. Billy Martin
    b. Lou Piniella
    c. Buck Showalter
    d. Joe McCarthy

20. Joe DiMaggio had a brother named Dom who played for the Red Sox.

    a. True
    b. False

QUIZ ANSWERS

1. C- 11 times

2. A – True

3. B- 2004

4. C – London

5. D- 0, they are both in the American League

6. B- David Ortiz

7. A – True

8. D- Dave Righetti

9. C – 1997

10. B- 1

11. C- Athletics

12. B – False

13. C – Bernie Williams

14. C- Jason Giambi

15. D- Harry Frazee

16. A- True

17. B- Cy Young

18. B – 6 times

19. D – Joe McCarthy

20. A – True

DID YOU KNOW?

1. The Yankees and Red Sox rivalry is one of the fiercest, oldest rivalries in all of American sports. They have been rivals for over 100 years.

2. There have been 4 different teams that have been a part of the Subway Series New York rivalry. Only two of those teams remain in New York, the other two have since moved to California.

3. Sparky Lyle is credited with being the first true "closer" in baseball. Lyle played for both the Red Sox and the Yankees.

4. In 1978, in a series against the Red Sox, the Yankees outscored Boston 42-9. This 4-game series played at Fenway Park became known as the "Boston Massacre."

5. Until interleague play started, the Yankees and Mets had only met in exhibition games that did not count towards regular season records. Since interleague play was introduced, the Yanks and Mets have played each other in the regular season every season since 1997. They also met in the 2000 World Series, which the Yankees won in 5 games.

6. In a controversial election, Nomar Garciaparra of the Red Sox started at shortstop for the American League in the 1999 MLB All-Star Game over Derek Jeter. A Red Sox fan had developed a computer program that allowed

Garciaparra to secure the win over Jeter. Both ended up playing in the game.

7. Many wonder when the Yankees-Red Sox rivalry began. It all began with the "Curse of the Bambino". Red Sox fans blamed their issues on the Yanks and Yankee fans rubbed it in their faces. The Red Sox did not win a World Series for another 85 seasons.

8. Yankees star, Don Mattingly went on to manage the former rival Dodgers. The Yankees were fierce rivals with the Dodgers when they were based in Brooklyn.

9. Sparkly Lyle, Roger Clemens, and Wade Boggs all left the Red Sox and went on to win a World Series with the Yankees.

10. During an ALCS game against the Red Sox, former Yankees coach, Don Zimmer was flipped onto the ground during a bench clearing brawl. The moment is one of the craziest moments documented amidst this heated rivalry.

CHAPTER 15:

THE AWARDS SECTION

QUIZ TIME!

1. How many times has a Yankee won the regular season American League MVP Award?

    a. 12
    b. 22
    c. 32
    d. 42

2. No Yankees manager has won the American League Manager of the Year Award in the 2000's.

    a. True
    b. False

3. Who was the first Yankees pitcher to win the Cy Young Award?

    a. Whitey Ford
    b. Sparky Lyle
    c. Bob Turley
    d. Ron Guidry

4. Which Yankee most recently won the Rookie of the Year Award?

    a. Derek Jeter
    b. Aaron Judge
    c. Gleyber Torres
    d. Dellin Betances

5. How many Gold Glove Awards did Don Mattingly accumulate during his playing career?

    a. 5
    b. 2
    c. 9
    d. 12

6. Three former Yankees won 5 Silver Slugger Awards total in their careers, which is tied for most in franchise history. Which player comes in 2nd in franchise history with 4 Silver Slugger Awards total in their career?

    a. Derek Jeter
    b. Jorge Posada
    c. Robinson Cano
    d. Dave Winfield

7. Derek Jeter won the Triple Crown in 2002.

    a. True
    b. False

8. Which Yankee pitcher won ALCS MVP in 2009?

    a. CC Sabathia
    b. AJ Burnett

c. Andy Pettitte

d. Joba Chamberlain

9. How many American League regular season MVP awards did Alex Rodriguez win as a member of the Yanks?

    a. 0

    b. 6

    c. 2

    d. 1

10. Which Yankee outfielder won the Wilson Defensive Player of the Year Award in 2016?

    a. Jacoby Ellsbury

    b. Brett Gardner

    c. Aaron Hicks

    d. Carlos Beltran

11. How many times did Derek Jeter win the Hank Aaron Award (for best hitters) in his career?

    a. 6

    b. 7

    c. 2

    d. 0

12. The 1996, 1998, and 2000 Yankees won the ESPY Award for "Outstanding Team".

    a. True

    b. False

13. Which Yankees player has been selected to the most MLB All-Star Games?

a. Derek Jeter

b. Babe Ruth

c. Yogi Berra

d. Mickey Mantle

14. The James P. Dawson Award is given to the rookie with the best performance at the end of Spring Training. Which Yankee won this award in 1988?

a. Al Leiter

b. Tommy John

c. Dave Righetti

d. Ron Guidry

15. How many "Best Coach/Manager" ESPY Awards did Joe Torre collect in his managerial career?

a. 0

b. 6

c. 4

d. 1

16. Derek Jeter was named Sports Illustrated's 'Sportsman of the Year' in 2009.

a. True

b. False

17. Which former Yankee was named the World Baseball Classic MVP in 2013?

a. Juan Cedeño

b. Pat Venditte

c. Walter Ibarra

d. Robinson Cano

18. Three Yankees were named to the Sports Illustrated Top 20 Male Athletes of the Decade in 2009. Which of the players below was NOT named to this list?

    a. Alex Rodriguez

    b. Andy Pettitte

    c. Mariano Rivera

    d. Derek Jeter

19. Which former Yankee was named the Associated Press Athlete of the Year in 1961?

    a. Yogi Berra

    b. Mickey Mantle

    c. Whitey Ford

    d. Roger Maris

20. Former Yankees broadcaster, Mel Allen won the first ever Ford C. Frick Award (presented to broadcasters for their impact left on the game of baseball) in 1978.

    a. True

    b. False

QUIZ ANSWERS

1. B – 22

2. A- True

3. C- Bob Turley

4. B- Aaron Judge

5. C- 9, the most in Yankees history

6. D- Dave Winfield

7. B – False

8. A- CC Sabathia

9. C- 2

10. B – Brett Gardner

11. C- 2

12. A- True

13. D – Mickey Mantle

14. A- Al Leiter

15. C – 4

16. A – True

17. D- Robinson Cano

18. B- Andy Pettitte

19. D- Roger Maris

20. A – True

DID YOU KNOW?

1. The New York Yankees have won 19 American League East Division titles, 40 American League pennants, and of course, 27 World Series championships. All of these are MLB records. This is what arguably makes the Yankees the most successful sports team in America.

2. Both Joe McCarthy and Casey Stengel won the Sporting News Manager of the Year Award three times in their managerial careers with the Yankees. McCarthy in 1926, 1938, and 1943. Stengel in 1949, 1953, and 1958. Bucky Harris, Ralph Houk, Bill Virdon, Buck Showalter, and Joe Torre have also won the award in their time as Yanks manager.

3. The Lou Gehrig Memorial Award is given to a MLB player who possess the same character as Gehrig both on the field and off. 5 Yankees have been given this award, including: Gil McDougald, Bobby Richardson, Tommy John, Don Mattingly, and Derek Jeter.

4. 5 Yankees have been awarded the Cy Young Award by the MLB, but USA Today also gives out Cy Young Awards. Mariano Rivera won a USA Today Cy Young Award in 2005 and CC Sabathia won one in 2010.

5. DHL gave out their Hometown Heroes Award in 2006. This award was presented to the most outstanding player in the history of each franchise. Babe Ruth was given the DHL Hometown Heroes Award for the Yankees.

6. The MLB Comeback Player of the Year Award was first presented in 2005. Jason Giambi won the very first Comeback Player of the Year Award for his re-emergence in the game during his time with the Yankees.

7. Don Mattingly holds the record for most Gold Glove Awards in Yankees history with 9. Ron Guidry and Derek Jeter are tied for second place with 5 each.

8. The most recent player to win AL Rookie of the Year for the Yankees is Aaron Judge in 2017. It had been over 20 years since a Yankee had won the award since Derek Jeter in 1996.

9. Derek Jeter won the Baseball America Minor League Player of the Year Award in 1994.

10. In 2009, the Yankees were named Sports Illustrated's 'Best MLB Franchise of the Decade.'

CHAPTER 16:

THE BRONX

QUIZ TIME!

1. What type of music originated in the Bronx?

    a. Country

    b. Rock

    c. Jazz

    d. Hip hop/rap

2. The Bronx is home to poet Edgar Allen Poe's final home.

    a. True

    b. False

3. Which celebrity is NOT from the Bronx?

    a. Jennifer Lopez

    b. Billy Joel

    c. Demi Lovato

    d. Regis Philbin

4. The Bronx is home to one of the world's largest zoos. What is the name of that zoo?

a. New York Zoo

b. Bronx Zoo

c. Ross Park Zoo

d. Bronx Wildlife Center

5. Standing over the Harlem River is the oldest bridge in NYC. What is its name?

a. Robert F. Kennedy Bridge

b. Whitestone Bridge

c. Hell Gate Bridge

d. High Bridge

6. Which is a popular nickname for the Bronx?

a. "B-Town"

b. "Boogie Down Bronx"

c. "Beautiful Bronx"

d. "B-City"

7. The Bronx is the birthplace of the word "hella."

a. True

b. False

8. Which dance style originated in the Bronx?

a. Ballet

b. Tap

c. Breakdancing

d. Rumba

9. What famous U.S. monument was carved in a vacant lot in the Bronx?

a. Statue of Liberty

b. Lincoln Memorial

c. Washington Monument

d. Vietnam Women's Memorial

10. The Bronx is home to America's oldest public golf course. What is its name?

a. Van Cortlandt Park Golf Course

b. Pelham Bay and Split Rock Golf Course

c. Clearview Park Golf Course

d. Dunwoodie Golf Course

11. What is the Bronx's motto?

a. "The sweetest place on Earth"

b. "Together for a better tomorrow"

c. "City of eternal sunshine"

d. "Yield not to evil"

12. The Bronx does not have a beach.

a. True

b. False

13. Which activity was popularized in the Bronx?

a. Stickball

b. Fencing

c. Archery

d. Handball

14. What is the name of Jennifer Lopez's popular song that references her love for the Bronx and appreciation for growing up there?

a. "On the Floor"

b. "Love Don't Cost a Thing"

c. "Jenny from the Block"

d. "Dance Again"

15. Which famous movie director is from the Bronx?

a. Penny Marshall

b. Clint Eastwood

c. Steven Spielberg

d. Quentin Tarantino

16. The Bronx is known as the greenest borough.

a. True

b. False

17. Which famous ice cream brand originated in the Bronx?

a. Blue Bunny

b. Dreyer's

c. Ben & Jerry's

d. Häagen-Dazs

18. Which former U.S. president called the Bronx home when he was a young boy in the 1920s?

a. Barack Obama

b. Bill Clinton

c. Richard Nixon

d. John F. Kennedy

19. Cuban singer Celia Cruz is buried at which Bronx cemetery?

a. Pelham Cemetery

b. St. Raymond Cemetery

c. Woodlawn Cemetery

d. Tulocay Cemetery

20. Belmont/Arthur Ave. is home to NYC's REAL Little Italy according to chef Rachael Ray.

a. True

b. False

QUIZ ANSWERS

1. D – Hip hop/rap

2. A – True

3. C – Demi Lovato

4. B – Bronx Zoo

5. D – High Bridge

6. B – "Boogie Down Bronx"

7. B – False, Oakland (Bay Area)

8. C – Breakdancing

9. B – Lincoln Memorial

10. A – Van Cortlandt Park Golf Course

11. D – "Yield not to evil"

12. B – False, Orchard Beach

13. A – Stickball

14. C – "Jenny from the Block"

15. A – Penny Marshall

16. A – True

17. D – Häagen-Dazs

18. D – John F. Kennedy

19. C – Woodlawn Cemetery

20. A – True

DID YOU KNOW?

1. The Bronx is 57 square miles total. It has a population of 1.5 million people. The name "Bronx" originated from Jonas Bronck, who established the first settlement in the area back in 1639.

2. In addition to breakdancing, salsa and mambo dancing also originated in the Bronx.

3. Before arriving in grocery stores across New York City, bananas are ripened in pressurized rooms at the Banana Distributors of NY warehouse in the Bronx.

4. America's first president, George Washington, stayed in the Van Cortlandt House during the American Revolution. It is now the oldest house in the Bronx.

5. The Bronx Museum of the Arts has over 800 works on display. They also have a section dedicated to artistic graffiti. Admission to the museum is completely free.

6. The Bronx Zoo is home to over 6,000 animals. It has a zoo, children's zoo, aquarium, and even a 4D theater.

7. The Bronx is home to The Hall of Fame of Great Americans. It was created in 1900 to honor Ben Franklin, Eli Whitney, and Mark Twain.

8. The Bronx Botanical Gardens contains over one million plants on 250 acres of space.

9. The Bronx River is the only freshwater river in New York City.

10. The famous film *The Godfather* was set in the Bronx.

CHAPTER 17:

THE BABE

QUIZ TIME!

1. Where was Babe Ruth born?

    a. San Francisco, California

    b. Tampa Bay, Florida

    c. Baltimore, Maryland

    d. Providence, Rhode Island

2. Babe Ruth liked to eat uncooked steaks.

    a. True

    b. False

3. Babe Ruth served jail time for _____.

    a. Speeding

    b. Stealing

    c. Vandalizing

    d. Fighting

4. In June of 1938, Babe Ruth was hired as a first base coach for which team?

a. New York Yankees

b. Boston Red Sox

c. Chicago Cubs

d. Brooklyn Dodgers

5. Babe Ruth often tucked a piece of what vegetable under his hat to keep him cool while playing?

a. Spinach

b. Zucchini

c. Cabbage

d. Cucumber

6. How many times did Babe Ruth steal home in his career?

a. 0 times

b. 2 times

c. 5 times

d. 10 times

7. Babe Ruth hated wearing underwear.

a. True

b. False

8. What was Babe Ruth's favorite thing to eat for breakfast?

a. 12 pancakes

b. 18-egg omelet

c. 10 waffles and bacon

d. 6 doughnuts and a cup of yogurt

9. How did Babe Ruth's father die?

a. Car accident

b. Heart attack

c. Family brawl

d. Cancer

10. Babe Ruth spoke what language besides English?

    a. Spanish

    b. French

    c. Italian

    d. German

11. How many home runs did Babe Ruth hit AGAINST the Yankees in his career?

    a. 12

    b. 34

    c. 59

    d. 90

12. Babe Ruth was one of the earliest athletes to hire a PR rep.

    a. True

    b. False

13. Babe Ruth was named Yankees captain in 1922. How many games did he hold the title for?

    a. 400

    b. 108

    c. 6

    d. 29

14. Babe Ruth lived the majority of his life believing his birthday was February 7, 1894. However, that was not correct. When was his real birthday?

    a. February 6, 1893

b. February 6, 1895

c. February 7, 1895

d. February 7, 1893

15. How did Babe Ruth pass away?

    a. Cancer

    b. Natural causes

    c. Heart attack

    d. Lou Gehrig's Disease

16. After he retired from baseball, Babe Ruth had a brief career in radio and film, then spent the rest of his life vacationing in Florida and golfing.

    a. True

    b. False

17. At the catholic school that Babe Ruth attended as a boy, each student was taught and trained for an industrial career. What was Babe Ruth trained to be?

    a. Construction worker

    b. Auto mechanic

    c. Factory worker

    d. Shirt maker

18. At Comiskey Park, during innings when Babe was not batting, he would cross the street and order_____ from a bar. Then he would head back to the game in time to either bat or get back out to the outfield.

    a. Hot dog and a beer

    b. Chicken nuggets and a root beer

    c. Garlic fries and a glass of wine

    d. Nachos and a beer

19. Babe is the only player with the last name "Ruth" in MLB history.

    a. True

    b. False

20. The Baby Ruth candy bar is named after Babe Ruth.

    a. True

    b. False

QUIZ ANSWERS

1. C – Baltimore, Maryland

2. A – True

3. A – Speeding

4. D – Brooklyn Dodgers

5. C – Cabbage

6. D – 10 times

7. A – True

8. B – 18-egg omelet

9. C – Family brawl

10. D – German

11. D – 90

12. A – True

13. C – 6, Babe attacked a heckler in the stands and was stripped of his title only six games later.

14. B – February 6, 1895

15. A – Cancer

16. A – True

17. D – Shirt maker

18. A – Hot dog and a beer

19. A – True

20. B – False, It is actually named after President Grover Cleveland's daughter, Ruth.

DID YOU KNOW?

1. It is widely believed that Babe Ruth was an orphan because he was sent to an orphanage when he was 7. That is not true, however. His parents sent him to an orphanage because Babe was such a troublemaker.

2. One day during a game at the Polo Grounds, Babe Ruth lost a fly ball in the sun in left field. After that, he refused to ever play left field in the sun again....and he didn't. Whether he played left or right field was determined by the geographical location of each ballpark from there on out.

3. During a game at Griffith Stadium, Babe Ruth knocked himself unconscious by running headfirst into a concrete wall while trying to catch a fly ball. He was out for five minutes total. He stayed in the game, went 3-for-3, hit two doubles, and played the second game of that day's doubleheader as well.

4. Babe Ruth once punched an umpire in the head during a game before being dragged off the field by police. It cost him a $100 fine.

5. Babe Ruth was the very first highest paid player in Major League Baseball.

6. Many know that Babe tended to refer to other people as "Kid" or "Doc." This is because he had a very hard time remembering names.

7. Babe desperately wanted to be a manager for an MLB team once he retired as a player. Many teams were hesitant to hire him, though, because of his partying reputation. So, he never got to manage.

8. Babe fell in love with baseball thanks to a monk at his school who introduced him to the sport.

9. Babe won three World Series with the Red Sox and four with the Yankees.

10. It is estimated that Babe had 58 different nicknames... including "Babe."

CHAPTER 18:

THE IRON HORSE

QUIZ TIME!

1. Where was Lou Gehrig born?

   a. Sioux Falls, South Dakota

   b. Seattle, Washington

   c. Yorkville, New York

   d. San Diego, California

2. Lou Gehrig never married.

   a. True

   b. False

3. What did Lou Gehrig major in at college?

   a. Journalism

   b. Education

   c. Business

   d. Engineering

4. How many colleges was Lou Gehrig recruited by thanks to his athletic abilities?

   a. 13

b. 18

c. 24

d. 32

5. Gehrig's mom was a cook/housekeeper. What did his dad do for a living?

    a. Auto mechanic

    b. Cook

    c. Metal worker

    d. Construction worker

6. During his 2,130-game playing streak, how many fractures did Lou Gehrig get in his hands?

    a. 3

    b. 10

    c. 17

    d. 23

7. Gehrig was the first athlete to have his number retired.

    a. True

    b. False

8. Lou Gehrig's parents were immigrants from _____.

    a. Poland

    b. Germany

    c. Italy

    d. Canada

9. After retirement from baseball, Gehrig was a civil worker for the City of New York. What did he determine in this job role?

a. If businesses were eligible for a building permit

b. When to re-pave popular roads across the city

c. Whether or not a child was being abused by their parent/s

d. The time of release for prisoners

10. What was Lou Gehrig's full name?

a. Henry Lou Gehrig

b. Louis Henry Gehrig

c. Harry Louis Gehrig

d. Henry Louis Gehrig

11. Gehrig starred in a Western film in which he played himself. What was the name of that movie?

a. Red River Range

b. Rawhide

c. Under the Western Stars

d. Overland Stage Raiders

12. A WWII ship was named after Lou Gehrig. On Gehrig's birthday, the ship landed at Normandy Beach, almost 2 weeks after D-Day.

a. True

b. False

13. Lou Gehrig auditioned to play which famous Hollywood film character?

a. Robin Hood

b. Ebenezer Scrooge

c. Tarzan

d. The Cowardly Lion

14. What holiday did Lou Gehrig's "Luckiest Man" speech take place on?

    a. Memorial Day
    b. 4th of July
    c. Labor Day
    d. Halloween

15. Lou Gehrig's Disease is also known as _____.

    a. ALT
    b. ATS
    c. GLS
    d. ALS

16. Lou Gehrig was once married to Marilyn Monroe.

    a. True
    b. False

17. We all know "The Iron Horse" was Gehrig's most popular nickname. Which nickname below did he NOT go by?

    a. Buster Gehrig
    b. Columbia Lou
    c. Go Yard Gehrig
    d. Biscuit Pants

18. President Franklin D. Roosevelt sent flowers to Eleanor after Lou passed away.

    a. True
    b. False

19. How many World Series did Gehrig win with the Yanks?

a. 3

b. 5

c. 6

d. 8

20. Lou was the only one of four kids to survive. He had siblings, but none of them survived infancy.

    a. True

    b. False

QUIZ ANSWERS

1. C – Yorkville, New York

2. B – False, He married Eleanor in 1933.

3. D – Engineering

4. C – 24

5. C – Metal worker

6. C – 17

7. A – True

8. B – Germany

9. D – The time of release for prisoners

10. D – Henry Louis Gehrig

11. B – *Rawhide*

12. A – True

13. C – Tarzan

14. B – 4th of July

15. D – ALS, Amyotrophic Lateral Sclerosis

16. B – False, Joe DiMaggio was once married to Marilyn Monroe.

17. C – Go Yard Gehrig

18. A – True

19. C – 6

20. A – True

DID YOU KNOW?

1. Lou Gehrig averaged 1 RBI per game during his career.

2. Lou and his wife Eleanor used a Ouija board that told them, "You will soon be called upon to face the most difficult problem of your life." They assumed it was about their potential adoption of a child. Signs of Lou's ALS began to show 8 days later.

3. Gehrig played the 1938 season with the onset of ALS. He kept slumping and had no idea why his body was fighting him. Even through the struggles of the disease, in his final season in baseball, Gehrig hit .295 with 29 home runs and 114 RBI.

4. Since ALS was so new when Gehrig was developing it, he had no idea he was going to die so young because of it. He assumed he would be forced to live his life in a wheelchair, but never believed he would die, even up to the very end.

5. Gehrig's mom desperately wanted him to become an engineer. She did not approve of her son's interest in baseball, which she called a sport for bums.

6. While in college, Gehrig played in the minors under the name "Henry Lewis" secretly. Since he was making money, this was against the rules. When Columbia found out, they suspended him for one season.

7. Lou Gehrig was born on June 19, 1903. He died in his sleep on June 2, 1941, just a couple weeks short of his 38th birthday.

8. Lou married Eleanor in a small ceremony at their apartment one early morning. After the wedding, the couple got a motorcycle police escort to Yankee Stadium where Lou played in a game.

9. Gary Cooper played Lou Gehrig in *The Pride of the Yankees*. The film came out the year after he died.

10. Gehrig never missed a single game from June 1925 through April 1939.

CONCLUSION

Learn anything new? Now you truly are the ultimate Yankees fan. Not only did you learn about the Yankees of the modern era, but you also expanded your knowledge back to the Highlander days.

You learned about the Yankees origins and their history, plus more about where they come from. You learned about the history of their uniforms and jersey numbers, you identified some famous quotes and read some of the craziest nicknames of all time. You focused on the life and legacy of the captain of all captains, the legendary Derek Jeter. You learned more about Yankee legends, Babe Ruth and Lou Gehrig. You acknowledged Yankees stats and recalled some of the most infamous Yankees trades and drafts. You broke down your knowledge by outfielders, infielders, pitchers, and catchers. You looked back on 27 World Series Championships and the awards that came with them. You also learned about the Yankees fiercest rivalries of all time including the infamous Yankees-Red Sox rivalry that began with the Curse of the Bambino.

Every team in the MLB has a storied history, but none of them have quite the depth that the Yankees do. Being the ultimate Yankees fan takes a lot of knowledge, which you tested with this book. Whether you knew every answer or made Babe Ruth roll over in his grave, you learned some of the most incredible history that the game of baseball has to offer.

The history of the Yankees represents what we all love about the game of baseball. The heart, the determination, the consistency, and the unexpected moments, plus the players that inspire us and encourage us to do our best because even if you get knocked down, there is always another game and another day.

With players like Aaron Judge, the future for the Yankees looks bright as usual There is no doubt that this franchise will continue to be one of the most iconic sports teams in the world. Those pinstripes are synonymous with winning, America, and the game of baseball in general.

It's a new decade, which means there is a clean slate, ready to continue writing the history of the New York Yankees. The ultimate Yankees fan cannot wait to see what's to come for their beloved Bronx Bombers.

Here's to the chase for No. 28, New York!

Made in the USA
Middletown, DE
26 February 2021